Getting Started in
Trading

The Getting Started In Series

Getting Started in Trading

Sunny J. Harris

John Wiley & Sons, Inc.

New York • Chichester • Weinheim • Brisbane • Singapore • Toronto

Library of Congress Cataloging-in-Publication Data
Harris, Sunny J.
    Getting started in trading/Sunny J. Harris.
        p.   cm.—(The Getting started in series)
    Includes bibliographical references (p.) and index.
    ISBN 0-471-39507-2 (pbk.: Alk. paper)
    1. Speculation. 2. Stocks. 3. Stock exchanges. I. Title. II. Getting started in.
    HG4521 .H313 2001
    332.64'5—dc21   00-043464

Printed in the United States of America.

10 9 8 7 6 5 4 3 2 1

This book is dedicated to my partner, Gina L. Maraio, who has stood by me and maintained the faith through thick and thin; to my daughter, Colby E. Littlejohn, who is my pride and joy as well as my understudy and right-hand woman; and to my mother, Mae B. Evans, whose strength I emulate. Above all, I thank Howard,* who is the inspiration and guidance in all that I do.

*From the children's prayer "Our Father Who art in Heaven, Howard be Thy name."

Well done is better than well said.
—Benjamin Franklin, *Poor Richard's Almanack*, 1737

Winners look for solutions—losers look for excuses.
—Adrienne Laris Toghraie

Contents

Appendix B

Foreword

The beginning stages of a trader's education sets the foundation for each new level of success. The level of success you achieve is determined by how you apply a good education. *Trading* gives a new trader the guidelines for developing the education necessary to begin trading.

Working as a traders' coach for the last 10 years, I have found that most excessive trading losses result from the bad habits traders develop at the beginning of their trading careers. Some of these bad habits are created because traders do not have:

- ✔ The basic fundamental knowledge of the trading industry and how all of its components interrelate
- ✔ A trading plan
- ✔ Rules they believe will give them good results
- ✔ A tested system
- ✔ Money management rules

Lack of discipline is the main reason traders fail. In order to be disciplined, you must trust your methodology and money management rules. If you have not developed the basic education necessary to be a good trader, you will not have the discipline necessary to follow your rules. If you do not follow your rules, you will not get profitable results. *Getting Started in Trading* will give you the education you need so you can trust your ability as a trader.

The five main reasons beginning traders do not start out with the basics needed for good trading are:

1. Their enthusiasm to trade immediately takes over without their giving thought to the possible consequences.
2. They do not know where to get the right information to start.
3. They find the method taught too difficult to understand.

4. They have information from too many sources, which causes them to go in too many directions at the same time.

5. They feel that to succeed they must establish complicated rules, which results in too many possible things that can go wrong.

Getting Started in Trading is easy to understand and easy to apply quickly, and will leave you with the confidence that you have the ability and knowledge to be a successful trader.

Sunny Harris is an extraordinary trader who was ranked the number one money manager in 1994 by Stark Research in the under-$10,000,000 category. She won that honor trading a system she developed that could only be for the kind of trader who can look death in the face and laugh. This system brought in 365 percent that year on investment dollars and fits the dynamo side of her personality. The second system she trades, which she also developed, is for traders with a pulse. This system brings in a very respectable, predictable, and safe 18 percent with 8.5 percent drawdown. This system satisfies her conservative side.

In addition to trading, Sunny publishes the *Traders' Catalog & Resource Guide*. She began this publication when it became general knowledge in the industry that she had been keeping a "black book" of sorts on everyone and everything in the business—from brokerages to software and weather. The word spread so far and wide about her "black book" that she was getting calls from all over the country. By April 1993 Sunny was putting together her first catalog. And that is how a great business idea was born.

While the *Traders' Catalog & Resource Guide* is the phone book directory combined with editorial magazine, *Getting Started in Trading* is the cookbook. The current publication is an alphabetical and a categorical listing of who's who. The latter is the step-by-step guide you need to get started.

As if trading and publishing were not enough to keep her busy, Sunny also teaches four outstanding, hands-on seminars per year, is finishing her Ph.D. in mathematics, and does private consultations with qualified traders.

There is a lot to be learned from the brilliant investing and trading successes of Sunny Harris. Her determination, her thoroughness, and her dedication to the techniques of trading and investing are an inspiration to all of us. And there is also a lot to be learned from her willingness to organize and catalog the entire world of trading and to share it with the rest of us.

Getting Started in Trading will give you the basic understanding of the trading business. It will save you time and money, and research effort, providing you with what is necessary to get started. *Getting Started in Trading* will be a continuous resource as you develop into a successful trader.

Sunny Harris's generosity to the investment world is a model of prosperity consciousness in action. Everyone seeking affluence in every part of their lives should follow her prosperity principle: "You only have what you give."

—Adrienne Laris Toghraie
April 2000

Preface

I am now a professional trader. I was not always a trader, nor did I plan to become one. I was not an economist or a broker, a banker or any other professional involved in the markets. I, like most other individual traders, came from a background unrelated to investing and trading.

In my *Trading 101* seminars, I always ask about my students' backgrounds and have found that many aspiring traders come from engineering, physics, and mathematics backgrounds, as do I. Recently I have found that a large percentage of my students are physicians. It seems to me a natural extension of logical abilities, but does not mean that one has to have a degree in math to be a trader. Yet a solid foundation of logical abilities does seem to be an absolute necessity for developing a theory, thoroughly testing the theory, and following the trading system once developed.

My formal education has been in mathematics. As a new mathematician straight out of graduate school, I abhorred the thought of using my training for any practical application like programming. But earning a living became a necessity, and I began programming in the aerospace industry. I quickly came to love the challenge and the opportunity to apply symbolic logic to the real world.

After an immensely successful entrepreneurial venture into computer graphics, I began the process of learning how to invest my own money. Early on I bought stocks and bonds, hired money managers, ventured into mutual funds and money market funds, and purchased real estate and a variety of limited partnerships. Most of these ventures were profitable, some very much so. At one point I lost $75,000 with a "sure-thing" commodities trader and swore I'd never have anything to do with futures trading again.

While my advisors invested my money, I monitored the efficacy of their advice by keeping data and charts on a weekly basis. The mechanics of this process taught me the basics of technical analysis, and I wanted to learn more.

At first I kept my charts by hand on a piece of 10×10 graph paper, and I got my data from *Investors Business Daily* and the *Wall Street Journal* each morning. Later I began watching FNN, the Financial News Network, from 6:00 a.m. each morning until the market closed at 1:15 p.m. California time.

The more I learned, the more I wanted to learn. I bought my first book on technical analysis, John Murphy's *Technical Analysis of the Futures Markets*, and dug in. After weeks of study, the pages of the book were nearly covered with fluorescent yellow from highlighting, so I purchased a second copy and studied some more. And, just before I took the Level II Chartered Market Technician exam last year, I read John Murphy's book again!

The more I studied, the more I feared that there was so much to learn that I had better leave money management to the professionals. But I was still curious.

As I kept my investment charts, I began keeping track of additional background charts: the Dow Jones Industrial Average, the dividends of the Dow, interest rates, and the price of gold. It was in this process that I began to see patterns and to understand some of the concepts in Murphy's work.

Initially, I observed that a parabolic curve usually collapses, that the dividend of the Dow tends to range between 3.0 and 6.0, and that the trend turns when the dividend stays too long at one extreme. In September of 1987 I saw these two conditions in the DJIA and decided to act. With over $1 million in equities and equity funds, I told my broker to liquidate. He disagreed. "This is the biggest bull run in history," he said. After a long lunch, at which I showed him my new-found technical analysis techniques, he still disagreed. Nevertheless, it was my money, so I liquidated and went to Europe on vacation.

When the market closed down 105 points on Friday, October 16, 1987, I stated firmly, "It'll drop 500 points on Monday. I can see it in the charts." From my hotel room in London I watched with excitement as the U. S. market collapsed on that fateful Black Monday. I decided then and there to pursue advanced education in technical analysis—vigilantly.

Over the next two years I consumed books and audio/videotapes on technical analysis. I attended every seminar I could find that even remotely touched on technical analysis. I voraciously read newsletters and watched FNN religiously. As I studied, I kept notes, and vowed to one day write a book so that other novices would not have to go through the same grueling process to learn about trading.

—Sunny J. Harris
April 2000

Getting Started in —
Trading

Chapter 1

In the Beginning . . .

This book, *Getting Started in Trading*, collects years of study and experimentation, condensed to an easy-to-use guide for the newcomer. *Getting Started in Trading* is like an overview class: You will learn about the existence of concepts but will not learn the concepts in depth. You will, however, learn where to look for information on each of these concepts, so that you may explore indepth and develop your knowledge base further if a particular topic appeals to you. I've drawn liberally from the work of others, using quotes and telling you where you can find more information on each subject.

Getting Started in Trading could have been subtitled "Everything You Ever Wanted to Know About Trading But Were Afraid to Ask," because we will be covering many very basic questions (and their answers) that students often are afraid to ask in a large class for fear of "sounding dumb."

There are thousands of professional money managers in the world: bankers, stock brokers, insurance brokers, real estate agents, art dealers, coin dealers, antique dealers, accountants, attorneys, and so on. Any one of these professionals will be happy to tell you that his or her specialty is the only one that will serve you well over the long term. In other words, they are all salespeople. Each of these professionals has one foremost goal: to increase his or her own take-home pay.

1

There is no such thing as altruism. We all have personal motives for doing good deeds, whether it is to gain attention, to seek rewards, or to earn money. For instance, I am not writing this book just for kicks and because I want to see you make a lot of money—I am writing it so you will purchase the book. As an aside, I am writing about a subject that I believe will assist you in making a lot of money. This is a trade: I get something of value and you get something of value. That is what this whole book is about, trading: the perceived fair exchange of one item or service for another item or service in the hopes that both parties benefit.

Getting Started in Trading is not for the aforementioned professionals—they already know it all. This book is written for everyone else. I will show you the ropes, pulling from many different resources. And I will introduce you to concepts that you may want to study indepth.

THE MARKET

trading
the act of buying and selling for speculation, as opposed to investing for the long term.

The market goes up and the market goes down. That is about all there is to it. Your job, as a trader, is to catch those swings at just the right time and price to profit from the movement.

Throughout this book, the word "market" refers to anything that one person wants to buy and another person wants to sell. If I have a car that I want to sell and you want to purchase, then that is the market.

The action of negotiating for the price at which we are willing to complete this transaction is called *trading*. Trading, when it involves more than two people, is an *auction* process.

auction
method for selling an asset to the highest bidder.

WHAT IS TRADING?

Trading is bartering; it is the exchange of goods or services. Trading has been part of human existence since the beginning of time. In fact, trading is truly the world's oldest profession. (Eve traded the apple for the knowledge of good and evil, didn't she?) Trading is not gambling, although some gamblers do trade.

Trading takes place when one person agrees to take the other person's eggs in exchange for vegetables. It happens when one barters two cows for a parcel of land. Trading also happens when you exchange coins for food. All traders have a commodity that they perceive to have a value. The exchange takes place when two parties agree that the value of each side of the trade is in parity.

If two traders do not agree that their commodities are of equal value, they will negotiate the quantities to be exchanged, until such time as they both are comfortable that the amounts to be traded are in parity. For instance, the trader with the land might want three cows to execute the trade, while the owner of the cows believes the land is only worth one cow. In this case, there is a spread between the *bid* and the *ask* prices.

The trader with the cows is only willing to bid one cow, while the trader with the land is asking three cows. There is a *spread* of two cows.

Ultimately, if the trade is to take place, the two traders will negotiate, until one of them increases the bid or lowers the ask price.

As time goes on and word gets around that these traders meet at a particular location to exchange wares, other people interested in bartering show up. Soon a marketplace exists. In one town it might be the cheese market, in another the fish market, but the exchange of one commodity for another commodity always is taking place.

The life of early traders became complicated. In order to supply their needs, they found themselves traveling from home with their cow, to the grain market where they traded the cow for more grain than they needed, on to the fish market where they traded part of the grain for some fish, and then to the egg market where they traded some of the grain for eggs, and then back home again with the grain, fish, and eggs. After some more negotiating with friends and neighbors, they agreed to create a *derivative*, which would make their lives easier. Thus, currency was born.

Early traders were able to take their currency to mar-

bid
offer to purchase something at a specified price. The bid price is the highest price any buyer is prepared to pay.

ask
an offer to sell something at a specified price. The asking price is the lowest price at which any seller is prepared to sell.

spread
the difference between the asking price and the bid price.

derivative
financial contract that does not necessarily have value of its own but whose perceived value is based on the value of the underlying instrument(s).

ket, negotiate the amount of currency to trade for the grain, fish, and eggs, and return home. The currency did not need a value of its own. All that was necessary was that all the trading parties agreed to make the trade based on the perceived underlying value of the currency.

The currency we use today in the United States is valueless. We carry around small pieces of paper with numbers on them and trade them at markets for other commodities that we want. Traders on the other side of the trade agree to take the pieces of paper because they believe the paper can be used in another market to make an exchange with someone else. The pieces of paper themselves do not have a value—only a perceived value.

Since our currency is no longer backed by gold or silver, you are no longer guaranteed the exchange of that paper for a fixed quantity of gold or silver. If a substantial number of traders began to doubt the value of the piece of paper, it would quickly become a worthless derivative. This same effect can happen with any derivative—traders can lose confidence in its value and the price will plummet. But for as long as we agree to bid and ask, trading will continue.

With each trade, the participants analyze their individual risk. Systematic traders will have analyzed the risk and measured it statistically against the possible reward. Discretionary (intuitive) traders will have measured their gut reaction to the impending trade.

Animals in nature trade without words. One animal kills the prey and allows several other to feed with it. Alpha animals snarl and growl at animals they don't want to trade with, and opposing animals must weigh the risk of confronting the alpha animal, compared with the reward of eating the food. This is known as the *risk/reward ratio*.

risk/ reward ratio
the relationship between the probability of loss and that of profit.

For instance, if you must put down $1,000 to make $500, the risk is pretty high. But if you can put down $1,000 to make $10,000, it looks pretty good.

However, you must consider the probability of winning before you actually know anything. What if, in the first example, the probability of winning is 50 percent— that is, for every two trades, one of them wins? But in the second example, where you could win $10,000, the probability of winning is 1 percent. Now which example looks better?

In Chapter 15 we'll take a closer look at the way you figure this out.

WHY DO *YOU* WANT TO TRADE?

Excuses

The Excitement Few endeavors challenge the excitement of putting your own money at risk. The success of Las Vegas and Atlantic City attests to this. Before currencies were invented, humans risked life and limb to prove their strength and courage. The Masai still expect young men to battle a lion as a rite of passage.

Nowadays we make more sophisticated wagers (bets), betting our hard-earned dollars at football games, horse races, and gaming tables. We revel in the excitement. We jump up and down and cheer for our side of the wager. Adrenaline surges through our bodies, our hearts pump faster. We love it!

This excitement can be extended to the investing arena. In fact, losing often can be more exciting than winning. The adrenaline high becomes its own reward. The determination to beat the market offers a challenge like no other.

The Challenge Demonstrating your prowess, like fighting the lion, is a personal quest designed to cull the weak from the strong in the survival-of-the-fittest game. It is part of our nature as humans to compete. We are designed to respond to the fight-or-flight adrenaline rush, but in modern time we have very few outlets for this response.

The markets are the combined demonstration of thousands of competitors entering into an anonymous fight for profit. The waves of price movement in the markets are the aftermath of a sometimes fiercely competitive auction. Bid and ask prices are simply evidence of two opposing parties arguing about how much something should cost.

The challenge for traders then becomes one of outsmarting the market. Novice and seasoned traders alike enter the game believing they can predict the next price move and, using the skills they bring to the arena (whether in mathematics, intuition, science, psychology, or logic), attempt to buy or sell at a price that has not yet been reached.

If you are interested in trading the markets for the challenge, find something else to do. Take your hunger for challenge and play backgammon or chess or football. Challenge the bully up the street to a fistfight. But forget about trading. Doing it for the challenge will lose your money.

Note: The market is always right. You will not outsmart the market consistently and over time. Eighty percent of the people who begin to trade the market today will not be trading in 12 months. And they will not quit because they were wise and took their profits to the bank. Eighty percent of them will lose their money to the 20 percent who trade with one consistent goal: **to make money.** This is the only goal that matters in trading.

Reasons

There is only one reason to trade: to make money. If you are trading the markets for any other reason, stop! Any other goal is simply an excuse to enter into the perceived excitement of the game.

Trading for the thrill is not a rational choice and usually is short-lived, because losing money generates just as much an adrenaline rush as making money. Trading without a business plan, without a clear-cut system, can be fun but dangerously costly.

The business of trading is boring if it's done right. The research and study, the testing and retesting of ideas, the consistent and unwavering following of your system does not create an adrenaline rush. The hard work and accomplishment does produce a feeling of satisfaction, when you have adhered to your rules over a long period of time and produced consistent results. You have a right to be proud of your work. But you will recognize when you are doing it correctly by the conspicuous *absence* of stress and adrenaline.

LEARNING THE JARGON

Every field has its own set of buzzwords that participants all seem to know and the people outside the field do not know. The only way I know to get acquainted with a new language is by total immersion. Reading the definitions that appear throughout this book will help you start learning key words and their meanings. Of course, it takes time, so if you forget one that was mentioned earlier, you can find it in the Glossary at the back.

When I first began trading, I had difficulty grasping the concept that you could sell something you did not own. It took repetition and acceptance for me to catch on to the concept of selling something short.

ADAGES

Old adages and wive's tales often have some basis in fact. In trading many sayings float around year after year, such as:

- ✔ Buy low, sell high.
- ✔ Let your profits run.
- ✔ Take small losses.
- ✔ Never let a win turn into a loss.
- ✔ The trend is your friend.
- ✔ Add to a winner, never to a loser.
- ✔ When in doubt, get out.

Some of these sayings are very true and should be posted on little yellow stickies on your computer monitor. Some, however, could not be further from the truth. The only way to learn which adages are useful for you is to test them. Test your theories to exhaustion and then follow your system. For instance, my system lets some winners turn into losses. That is the way the system works. If I were to try to second-guess the system, I would create a lot of small losses and a lot of *small* wins. Traders usually depend on small losses and big wins, so in this case the adage does not apply.

"When in doubt, get out" is another erroneous adage. You will always be in doubt! Trading takes discipline and nerves of steel. The only way to circumvent this natural emotion is to only trade a system that has been thoroughly tested and proven.

There are many more words of wisdom that traders of all kinds will be willing to share with you. Don't believe them. Don't believe anything until you have tested it. (See Chapter 15.)

The most important adages for you to remember go like this:

✔ Anything that sounds too good to be true, usually is.
✔ There is no such thing as a free lunch.
✔ You get what you pay for.

Remember to invest in your education. You would not wake up one morning and say "Today I'm a surgeon." You do not have the training for it. Why would you wake up one morning and say that you are a trader without the training?

For some strange reason, people throw their money at the markets without training and sufficient study. It has been observed that 80 to 90 percent of the people who begin trading today will have lost all their trading capital within the first 12 months and will quit trading. I think I know who they are. They are the ones without a proven system.

Remember, when you begin trading you are pitting yourself against the pros. They are there to take your money. And they will do it quickly unless you have prepared yourself as well as they have. You are stepping into the ring with the world heavyweight champion!

EXCHANGES

There are more than 140 financial *exchanges* around the world, some large and some very small. Let's stick with the main U.S. exchanges:

exchange
association of persons engaged in the business of buying and selling stocks, futures, and/or options.

New York Stock Exchange (NYSE)	www.nyce.com
New York Mercantile Exchange (NYME)	www.nymex.com
Chicago Mercantile Exchange (CME)	www.cme.com
Chicago Board of Trade (CBOT)	www.cbot.com
Chicago Board Options Exchange (CBOE)	www.cboe.com
Kansas City Board of Trade (KCBT)	www.kcbt.com
New York Board of Trade (NYBOT)	www.nybot.com
Nasdaq-Amex (NASD)	www.nasdaq-amex.com

The New York Stock Exchange had its beginnings in 1792, when 24 merchants and auctioneers met outdoors under a buttonwood tree on Wall Street. Countries older than ours had cheese markets, flower markets, gold markets, spice markets, and the like, which had specific gathering places and times at which to auction their wares. These were all exchanges.

Traditionally, futures trading takes place in *pits*. (See Figure 1.1.)

pit
a specially constructed arena (usually circular) on the trading floor of exchanges where trading is conducted. Some exchanges call these area rings rather than pits.

Pits usually are constructed with risers, making the inside ring lower than the outside rings, so that people on the outermost edge can see over the people standing in front of them. What appears to be pandemonium is really an open outcry auction taking place, with the sale going to the highest bidder and purchased from the lowest offerer. Supply and demand determines prices, sort of. Actually, fear and greed determine prices. When people all

FIGURE 1.1 The pit.

want something that someone else has, greed drives prices up. Conversely, when people are afraid of something losing its perceived value, they all try to get rid of it, at cheaper and cheaper prices. Successful trading takes into account the mathematics of human emotion.

Around the pits are banks of trading posts and telephones, where various firms locate their *floor brokers*. These floor brokers use hand signals to let the people in the pit know what they want to trade and for how much. The folks in the pit signal back when the deal is made, relaying the price at which the transaction took place. After each deal, a reporter places specially marked cards into a reporting device that records the transaction and causes it to appear on the ticker almost instantly.

The New York Stock Exchange works differently. Instead of an open outcry system, it is a specialist system. In this system, each stock is assigned a specialist firm through which all orders flow. The specialists keep what are called *limit order* books in which they line up buyers and sellers at their various price levels. Besides ordering the market, specialists also are charged with the responsibility of creating liquidity when otherwise there would be none. They do this by taking the other side of unmatched trades and either add to or deplete their inventory. This role theoretically adds stability to the market.

In the very near future, this sort of hectic activity will cease to exist, as the U.S. joins the rest of the world in creating completely electronic exchanges. Nevertheless, I think it is important to understand the history.

floor broker (FB) individual who executes any orders for the purchase or sale of any commodity futures or options contract on any contract market for any other person.

limit order order to buy or sell when a trade in the market occurs at a predetermined price.

One example of an electronic exchange in the U.S. is the Nasdaq market. Growing exponentially in popularity (and volume) in recent years, the Nasdaq is a virtual exchange that operates under a market maker system. This means that there is no "floor," only a decentralized network of computers that displays bids and offers of licensed market makers and routes trades appropriately. A market maker is essentially a firm charged with making a two-sided market by always stating a firm bid *and* offer on a certain number of shares in the given security.

READING THE TICKER TAPE

While ticker tapes were once a long strip of paper coming out of a bubble-shaped device (one of the many inventions of Alexander Graham Bell), for the most part they are now all digital electronics. Nevertheless, we still call it a tape. (See Figure 1.2.)

Each trade that takes place in the pits is echoed on the tape in shorthand, with its corresponding ticker symbol, the price at which the transaction happened, and how many shares were traded. Stock trades that take place in multiples of 100 shares are called *round lots*. Stock trades which are not multiples of 100 shares are called *odd lots*.

round lot order of shares in a multiple of 100.

odd lot order of shares that is not a multiple of 100.

Even though all these transactions are recorded on huge, state-of-the-art computers, the verbal auction sometimes takes place faster than clerks can report them. Then we say that the market got ahead of the tape. In fact, the clerks are just behind in their paperwork. If all trading

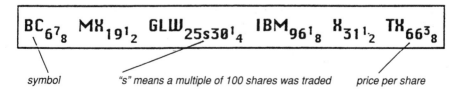

BC_{67_8} MX_{191_2} GLW_{25s301_4} IBM_{961_8} X_{311_2} TX_{663_8}

symbol   "s" means a multiple of 100 shares was traded   price per share

FIGURE 1.2 The ticker tape.

took place electronically, rather than in open outcry auctions, the market could not get ahead of the tape.

MARGIN

In stock trading, you may borrow up to half the price of the stock, usually against your account's total value, so that you may buy more stock than you would with cash only. For instance, if shares of XYZ stock are $100 each, you would pay $10,000 cash for 100 shares. If you *margined* the stock at 50 percent, you purchase 200 shares for the same $10,000.

The added leverage is to your benefit if the stock moves in your favor: You will make twice the profit. However, if the stock moves against you, you will have twice the loss.

Using margin is like buying a house with credit. You put down 20 percent of the price of the house; the bank lends you the rest.

If housing prices decline and you have to sell your house, you still will have to pay off the bank, even if your house sells for less than you paid for it. Even if your house burns down, you will still have to pay off the bank. But if housing prices rise before you sell your house, the profit you realize will be measured against your down payment, not against the full price of the house, so you make a higher rate of return.

This relationship is even more evident in futures trading, where the margin requirements are much lower. For instance, if the Standard & Poor's (S&P) 500 index is trading at 1500, one share each of 500 stocks is worth an index multiplier of $250, times the index value of 1500, giving a current value of $375,000. Yet at current margin levels, you can trade one contract with a $25,000 deposit. That's only a 7 percent margin requirement. If you purchase a contract and the value goes up, your profit is measured against your initial margin, a larger percentage than if you had paid cash. Again, if the contract decreases in value, you have lost a greater percentage than if you had

margin
in stock trading, an account in which purchase of stock may be financed with borrowed money; in futures trading, the deposit placed with the clearing house to assure fulfillment of the contract. This amount varies with market volatility and is settled in cash.

paid cash. And in the unlikely event that the S&P dropped to zero, you would be responsible for the full $375,000.

When determining whether to use margin, you must evaluate the risk vs. the reward. I look at worst cases when evaluating risk. What is the worst percentage drop the market has ever had? From a high of about 380 in 1929 to a low of about 40 in 1932 is almost a 90 percent drop. From a high of roughly 2,600 to a low of roughly 1,900 in 1987 is just about a 27 percent drop. Then I look at the probability of the worst case happening. How many times in history has the market experienced a decline of more than 27 percent? What is the average decline? How often do declines of this size take place? Only after I understand the risk do I begin to evaluate reward strategies.

FURTHER READING

For a light look at the basics of getting started, read *The Wall Street Journal Guide to Understanding Money & Markets*. For specific information about exchanges and exchange products, check at their web sites.

In *The New Contrarian Investment Strategy*, David Dreman does a fantastic job of giving an overview of and introduction to trading. Published in 1980, this book is as true today as it was then. Dreman's commonsense, practical approach makes this book must reading for beginners.

Of course, other books in the *Getting Started In* series are of enormous help.

Chapter

2

Approaches

FUNDAMENTAL ANALYSIS

fundamental analysis
analytical method by which only the sales, earnings, and value of a given tradable's assets may be considered. This theory holds that stock market activity may be predicted by looking at the relative data and statistics of a stock as well as the management of the company in question and its earnings.

Fundamental analysis relies on the study of reports to predict price trends; it addresses what a stock *should* sell for. In trading stocks, for instance, fundamental analysts rely on quarterly earnings reports; they look at reports about the company's products and personnel; they study reports about that sector of the economy and that industry in general.

To my mind, these are all just reports generated by humans striving to create a picture that satisfies their boss, or the board of directors, or their stockholders. I've been on boards of directors. I know what happens in those meetings. That's why I rely strictly on technical analysis.

Quoting from Steven Achelis in *Technical Analysis from A to Z:* "If we were all totally logical and could separate our emotions from our investment decisions, then fundamental analysis, the determination of price based on future earnings, would work magnificently. And since we would all have the same completely logical expectations, prices would change only when quarterly reports or relevant news was released."

Fundamental analysts study other trading vehicles in addition to stocks. They trade commodities, currencies, and interest rates as well. Some futures contracts move according to fundamental information. Soybean crops are affected by rain and lack of rain; the price of pigs and cows is affected by the price of their feed.

So, let's cover the fundamental analysis topics and see where we can find the information we would need as fundamental analysts.

Economic Indicators

Professional fundamental analysts regularly watch eight statistics.

1. *Leading Indicators* This monthly composite of 12 indicators is released by the Commerce Department's Bureau of Economic Analysis. Some believe that this index shows where the economy will be six months from now. The S&P 500 index is itself one of the leading indicators. Others include housing starts and orders for business equipment.

2. *Real GDP* (gross domestic product, formerly gross national product) The Commerce Department releases both projections and retrospective numbers for each quarter's inflation-adjusted GDP.

3. *Unemployment*

4. *Labor Costs* One measure is the employment cost index, which is calculated quarterly by the Bureau of Labor Statistics and reported in the *Wall Street Journal*.

5. *Productivity* Hourly worker productivity affects inflation. When productivity is improving, companies can afford to pay their workers more without having to recover all those increases through price increases.

6. *Inventory* If sales fail to materialize, excess inventory has to be reduced. Companies then buy fewer new items, thereby slowing the economy. The Commerce Department issues a ratio in the

middle of each month comparing the dollar value of business inventory nationally with sales.

7. *The Dollar* A strong dollar encourages cheap imports, holding inflation down but hurting certain U.S. industries that depend on exporting. A weakening dollar helps U.S. manufacturers but may encourage inflation.

8. *Interest Rates* The Federal Reserve tries to push rates down to stimulate the economy and raise them when it is growing too fast. The Fed puts its policy into effect chiefly by setting the level of short-term interest rates. When short-term rates are higher than long-term rates, it means the Fed is trying to slow business activity; when short-term rates are lower, the Fed is trying to speed up the economy.

Pick up a copy of Michael Sivy's *Money Guide—The Stock Market*. Sivy writes several of the chapters in this informative and basic book on investing, and it is well worth reading.

Analysis of Economic Data

Basic rules of thumb are kind of like adages; they work sometimes. As with any theory, my advice to you is always "Test it!" That said, Table 2.1 gives you a quick start for fundamental analysis that includes economic indicators.

Sources of Fundamental Data

Investors Business Daily (IBD) frequently runs a section called "Investor's NewsWire." While this section is actually advertorial in nature, it is devoted to corporate announcements. In Section A *IBD* supplies earnings news, new issues, and psychological data. Section B of *IBD* covers "The Economy" and includes reports on economic data and corporate news. All of these are fundamental in nature.

Table 2.1   Economic Indicators

Activity	Anticipated direction of the Market
Fed Raises Discount Rate	↓
An increase in the borrowing rate for banks usually results in increased rates for customers. Slows credit expansion.	
Money Supply Increases	↓
Excess money supply growth potentially can cause inflation and generate fears that the Fed may tighten money growth by allowing Fed funds rates to rise, which, in turn, lowers futures prices.	
Fed Does Repurchase Agreement	↑
The Fed puts money into banking system by purchasing collateral and agreeing to resell later. This helps bring rates down.	
Fed Does Reverses or Matched Sales	↓
The Fed takes money from the system by selling collateral and agreeing to repurchase at a later date. This decrease in money supply generally raises interest rates.	
Fed Buys Bills	↑
The Fed permanently adds to banking system reserves, which may cause interest rates to drop.	
Consumer Price Index Rises	↓
Rising inflation.	
Durable Goods Orders Rise	↓
Pickup in business activity usually leads to increased credit demand.	
Gross Domestic Product Falls	↑
Slowing economy. The Fed may loosen the money supply, prompting decline in interest rates.	
Housing Starts Rise	↓
Growth in economy and increased credit demand. The Fed is less accommodating and may attempt tightening by allowing rates to rise.	

Table 2.1 *Continued*	
Activity	*Anticipated direction of the Market*
Industrial Production Falls	↑
Slowing economy. The Fed may allow interest rates to fall to stimulate the economy.	
Inventories Up	↑
The economy is slowing since sales are not keeping up with production.	
Leading Indicators Up	↓
Strength in the economy leads to greater credit demand.	
Oil Prices Fall	↑
Reduces upward pressure on interest rates, enhancing prices of debt securities.	
Personal Income Rises	↓
Higher income equals more consumption, which equals increased demand and higher prices for consumer goods.	
Precious Metals Prices Fall	↑
Decreased inflation. Demand for inflation hedges abates.	
Producer Price Index Rises	↓
Rising inflation. Demand for goods rises as do prices. Investors require higher rates of return, pushing rates up.	
Retail Rates Rise	↓
Stronger economic growth. The Fed may have to tighten.	
Unemployment Rises	↑
Slow economic growth. The Fed may ease credit, causing rates to drop.	

Most of the online services such as America Online and CompuServe, provide both historical information and projections on fundamental data. The Internet is a great place to find fundamental data. Using the myriad of search engines, some of which are listed here, you can find thousands of references to fundamental data.

Search Engines

www.alltheweb.com

www.altavista.com

www.ask.com

www.excite.com

www.google.com

www.hotbot.com

www.infoseek.com

www.lycos.com

www.yahoo.com

Alternately, you can visit my web site www.money-mentor.com where I have a section on fundamental data that gives links to the most salient sites, along with a description of the information they provide. To find my section on fundamental data, just click on [INDEX] from the top menu bar and look under F. And, if that is not enough, click on [INDEX] and go to S, for Search Engines.

As an example of using an online service to find fundamental information, get on the web and go to www.yahoo.com. From the front page of that site you will see a list of categories from which to choose your interest. Click on [Business & Economy]. You will find that you have cascaded down one level to another set of categories. Now click on [Economics] or [Finance and Investment]. Now have fun! There is more information here than you can ever finish viewing, including stock reports, financial statements, earnings estimates, Edgar's 10Ks, stock market details, international markets, commodities, money and currencies, and economic indicators.

In addition to using search engines and roaming around the web, government bulletin board services supply fundamental data. Chapter 3 helps you find some of those.

What Should You Read?

Take a look at *Theory and Problems of Principles of Economics* by Dominick Salvatore and Eugene A. Diulio, if you want a quick overview of fundamentals. This book is straightforward and uses the format of Schaum's Outline Series: right to the point without a lot of verbiage.

For a more in-depth study of fundamentals, I suggest *Using Economic Indicators to Improve Investment Analysis* by Evelina Tainer.

If you look at these books and balk at the amount of work you are going to have to do to become a trader, find another profession. This is not a quick and easy process; it takes years of study and devotion. When you put your money on the line, you will be competing with professional traders who have spent their lives learning how to trade. Don't show up unprepared.

TECHNICAL ANALYSIS

Technical analysis is the study of prices. Technical analysts study supply and demand for securities and commodities based on trading price and volume. Using charts and modeling techniques, technicians attempt to identify price trends in a market. (See Figure 2.1.)

My research leads me to believe that all the information I will ever need is in price. The price of the underlying instrument already reflects opinion, rumor, volume,

> **technical analysis**
> form of market analysis that studies supply and demand for securities and commodities based on trading price and volume studies. Using charts and modeling techniques, technicians attempt to identify price trends in a market.

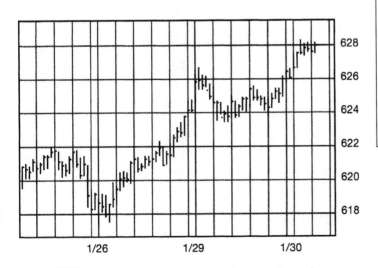

FIGURE 2.1 A chart is worth a thousand numbers.

volatility, news, and fundamentals, before it ever gets to my computer screen. Generally, technical analysts use charts of price to learn about price behavior and price patterns, but this is not always so. Some great technical analysts never look at a chart but rather do their analysis on the numbers alone.

Consider the following list of prices: 619.50, 620.10, 620.20, 620.10, 621.05, 621.30, 620.65, 620.80, 621.30, 621.10, 621.30, 621.65.

Do you see anything? I don't.

The number sequence just listed is found in the center of the chart in Figure 2.1. Now I can see several things: an uptrend, a range, a *trend line*, and a bounce. Whether you chart by hand or using a computer, technical analysis is easier with a picture.

trend line
straight line on a chart that shows the market's direction.

TIME FRAMES

The time frame in which you trade will be determined by several factors. First and foremost, what is your day job? How do you support yourself while you are learning to be a successful trader? If you are retired and independently wealthy, you can trade in any time frame you like; if you work from nine to five, then you had better trade with *end-of-day data* in a longer time frame than if you could watch the market minute by minute all day long.

Second, what is your nature? Are you an adrenaline junkie who drinks lots of coffee and cannot wait for the next challenge, or are you mellow and prefer a life of relaxation and no hassles?

Next you must consider the nature of the market you want to trade. Each market has its own rhythm. Some markets ask to be traded intraday and often; some reveal only a few good trades each year.

end-of-day data
data based on the closing price for the day. Often these data contain the open, high, and low for the day as well.

LONG TERM VS. SHORT TERM

Beginning traders often want to know just exactly how many days or months constitute long term. To me, these terms are both relative. Long term in my personal trading is about three days. If I hold a position that long, it is approaching a record length trade in my system. Yet if I were a bond trader and made trades weekly instead of hourly, long term would be a matter of months. In real estate ventures, what's long term? Years.

Nevertheless, to most people long term seems to mean months to years, intermediate term is weeks to months, and short term is hours to weeks.

REAL-TIME VERSUS END-OF-DAY DATA

Let's answer the easier question first. You may collect your data daily or weekly or historically, but if it includes closing prices for the day and not prices during the day, then it's end-of-day data. You can get these data from many vendors as well as from online services. Usually you will download it into your computer over a modem or read it in from a CD. Some vendors have their own bulletin board services from which you can purchase end-of-day data, and some even have special transmitters that send the data to you over an FM radio signal through cable TV signals and over the Internet.

real-time data

data regarding bid, ask, time, and sales, that are transmitted as they happen.

Real-time data are data you receive while they are happening. The only delay you should experience in these data is the amount of time it takes for transmission—just a few seconds at the most (if there is a floor). Of course, that is in an ideal world. Practically speaking, there is the additional delay for data entry on the floor of the exchange. When things get hectic in fast-moving markets, the data entry clerks cannot keep up with the transactions as fast as they happen. Then even real-time data feeds fall behind what is really happening on the floor. And when the market is moving really, really fast, it is next to impossible to phone your broker. That is when I step aside; I cannot trade without data, so I get out of the market until the data are available once again on a real-time basis.

To receive real-time data, you need a special feed from a vendor to transmit the data to you. In addition, you need permission from each exchange to receive the data. Of course, this means you will pay the exchange a fee for that permission. Some data vendors use special equipment, such as a satellite dish for your cable TV box, but many are now making their real-time data available over the Internet. The fees for real-time data have dropped dramatically in the last two years, to the point that often the exchange fees outweigh the vendor's fee. Contact each data vendor about the transmission methods used and fees.

Sources of Information and Data

Nowhere is the adage "you get what you pay for" more true than in the acquisition of data. Your trading decisions are directly influenced by the accuracy of your data. If you think you will save money by collecting you own data, or by finding a free source on the Internet, or by paying some discounted price for shareware, *forget it*. And don't trade data with your buddies.

The money you lose by making bad decisions with bad data will far outweigh any savings you made on the purchase of cheap data. As with any business tool, buy the best you can afford.

You are trading to make money. This is a business. You are a capitalist. As a capitalist you must pay for the goods and services you receive, to keep other capitalists providing those goods and services. This business is market driven, like the software business. If you pay people to do good work, they will do it; otherwise you will be whining that you have bad data and can not make good trading decisions. Data are available somewhere on almost anything. The data must be input and maintained by someone, and you will get what you pay for.

BULLETIN BOARDS

Bulletin board services (BBSs) are often small enterprises maintained (loosely) by a single individual. Some, on the other hand, are corporate or government in nature and have financial backing. Many of the small services come and go within weeks or months. Often a local weekly computer paper will list other BBS numbers in the back.

Many BBSs maintain collections of information that you can download for free. This can be a way to get started and to discover if you enjoy the process of research before you begin trading. Data acquired for free should not be relied on to make trading decisions but can be a useful practice tool.

 moving average
mathematical transform that is the sum of the current value plus ($n - 1$) previous values divided by n. The result smooths fluctuations in the raw data.

price/ earnings ratio (PE)
price of the stock, divided by earnings per share reported over the last four quarters.

CHART SERVICES

If you still do not have, or do not want to get, your own computer and data, fear not. You still can do a tremendous amount of technical analysis of charts that others have produced for you. Charting services sometimes fax you, but more often they mail charts of almost any and all stocks and commodities. You can get long-term and short-term charts on a daily, weekly, or monthly basis. Most of these services overlay the charts with a *moving average* or sometimes additional technical indicators, and usually show volume, *price/earnings ratios*, yields dividends, and shares outstanding.

Commodity Trend Service of Palm Beach Gardens, Florida, (800) 331-1069, provides chart books for futures, futures options, long-term charts, and nightly fax chart services.

BRIDGE CRB of Chicago, Illinois, (800) 621-5271, provides a wealth of weekly and monthly chart services as well as long-term publications such as *Futures, Perspective, CRB Commodity Yearbook,* and *Historical Wall Charts.*

M.C. Horsey & Company, Inc. of Salisbury, Maryland, (410) 742-3700, publishes *The Stock Picture* six times per year with 10 charts per page, 204 pages.

Mansfield Stock Chart Service of Jersey City, New Jersey, (201) 795-0629, publishes *OTC I, OTC II,* and *OTC III* weekly with nine charts per page, 267 pages.

The Value Line Investment Survey provides over 2,000 pages of information on stocks, including a long-term chart at the top of each page. The information is fundamental in nature but still provides a comprehensive long-term view of each stock. This tome is published by Value Line Publishing of New York, NY, (800) 624-3583.

Investor's Business Daily provides *Daily Graphs* at www.dailygraphs.com. Formerly a print product, the electronic version provides plenty of functionality.

COMMERCIAL DATA VENDORS

Bonneville Market Information (BMI)
(800) 424-5475
BMI offers over 110,000 real-time and delayed quotes on equities, bonds, futures, options, mutual funds and indices, along with a variety of informative news and weather services through FM, cable, satellite, and Internet services.

Commodity Systems, Inc. (CSI)
(800) 274-4727
CSI provides daily updates and historical data on commodities, stocks, options, indexes, and mutual funds.

Data Broadcasting Corp. (DBC)
(800) 527-0722 x719
DBC is the nation's leader in providing real-time market data to the individual investor. DBC transmits quotes on over 65,000 stocks, options, and commodities. The eSignal Program brings quotes to your computer via the Internet.

Data Transmission Network Corp. (DTN)
(800) 336-1818
DTN offers real-time quotes on stocks, options, and bonds, index as well as quotes on mutual funds, futures, precious metals, and a business news service.

Dial/Data
(800) 275-5544
Since 1972 leading institutional investors and thousands of individuals have relied on Dial/Data for its industry-standard database of daily and historical securities prices for U. S., Canadian, European, and Pacific Rim exchange-traded equities, futures, equity options, mutual funds, bonds, government issues, money markets, indices, and stock dividends.

Genesis Financial Data Services
(800) 808-3282
Genesis offers two data packages: historical data from 1968 on 140+ commodities and historical data from 1970 on 8,000 stocks. With the package you get their Navigator data management software, which allows you to convert the data into more than 20 formats.

Prophet Information Services Inc.
(800) 772-8040
Prophet gives you historical data back to 1968, customized updating capability, high-speed modem access, and a vast selection of stocks and futures from around the world.

Telerate Systems, Inc.
(201) 938-4000
Telerate offers dial-up modem access to their global information network.

Telescan, Inc.
(800) 324-8246
Telescan has current and historical quotes on stocks, mutual funds, indexes, and options, which you can import to spreadsheet and charting programs.

Tick Data, Inc.
(800) 822-8425
Tick Data has historical data on a tick-by-tick or daily basis. They also have a dial-up end-of-day updating service for both the daily and tick data.

Track Data
(800) 367-5968
Track Data provides real-time market data, financial databases, historical information, analytical services, and data manipulation tools.

MAGAZINES

Most magazines are not a source of timely trading data. It takes six weeks to publish and mail a magazine, so the data are stale by the time they get to you. Nevertheless, there are a few pieces of valuable data to be gleaned from the following magazines:

Technical Analysis of Stocks and Commodities publishes a table of trading liquidity for futures, which is essential to you as a trader in this respect: If the market you are trading is not liquid, you will be stuck on the wrong side of a trade at some point and not be able to get out. My advice to you is: Only trade those markets with high liquidity.

Futures magazine publishes a calendar that is a source of fundamental data, of a sort. Contract expirations, economic reports, and earning reports can affect short-term price fluctuations. If you want to know when these events are about to happen, check the calendar in the back of *Futures*.

In the same magazine you usually can find a table of data comparing the performance of top *commodity trading advisors* and *commodity pool operators*. If you are looking for someone to manage your money, start your quest by checking *Futures'* "Managed Money Review."

While you do not really find data in magazines, you will find advertisements for companies that will sell you data. Magazine ads are, in fact, your way of staying in

commodity trading advisor (CTA)
individual or organization that, for compensation or profit, directly or indirectly advises others as to the value or the advisability of buying or selling futures contracts or commodity options.

commodity pool operator (CPO)
individual or organization that operates or solicits funds for a commodity pool.

touch with the leading edge of technology. When a new data service emerges, it will be advertising its wares.

NEWSPAPERS

Barron's is a weekly publication of Dow Jones & Company, Inc., (800) 328-6800, appearing in the format all newspapers should adopt: It folds out like a big magazine so you can read it on the train or airplane with someone sitting next to you. The "Market Week" section of *Barron's* is chock full of data on stocks (U.S. and foreign), bonds, mutual funds, closed-end funds, money market funds, variable annuities, options, stock indices, futures, economic indicators, and charts.

In addition to an enormous variety of other information, *Consensus—National Futures and Financial Weekly* published by Consensus, Inc. of Kansas City, MO (816) 471-3862, (consensus—inc.com), provides comprehensive charting of all actively traded futures.

Investor's Business Daily, (800) 831-2525, published daily except weekends and holidays, is the most data-oriented newspaper. *IBD* starts right out with tables of data: Amex, bonds, credit markets, dividends, earnings, futures, industry groups, markets charts, money rates, mutual funds, Nasdaq OTC, national markets, new highs and lows, new issues, NYSE, options, and world markets.

The Wall Street Journal, (800) 451-5200, also a publication of Dow Jones & Company, Inc., is published daily except for weekends and holidays. This one you need a big desk for, but the "Money and Investing" section gives you daily data on money rates, municipal bonds, mutual funds, stocks, new issues, bonds, NYSE highs and lows, odd-lot trading, program trading, treasury issues, regional markets, and world markets.

ONLINE SERVICES

Each of the online services offers a wide variety of data, some free (except for the price of your membership to the service), some for a fee.

The main subscription/membership online services are:

America Online (AOL)
www.aol.com (800) 827-6364

CompuServe
www.compuserve.com (614) 457-8600

Dow Jones
www.dowjones.com (800) 815-5100

THE INTERNET

In addition to membership services that charge a monthly fee, there is the Internet. Mysterious as it is to some, the Internet is our only avenue of free speech, so far. The Internet is not administered by any single company or governing body; it is true anarchy. As such, the information content is left to the whim (and profitability) of the individual provider.

The Internet is the name we give to the pipelines that connect thousands and thousands of computers around the world via modems and phone lines. Each networked computer has a unique address, like 123.456.789.123, that functions rather like a zip code. When one computer wants to find another, it just needs the proper address. Various software vendors make software browsers available that allow you to assign names you can remember to these addresses and that makes it easy to search many, many computers for information. The most popular browsers are Netscape and Microsoft's Internet Explorer.

Furthermore, most of the commercial online services offer a link to the Internet. You simply log on to your online service (i.e., AOL) and click the Internet button.

The only problem then is that to find information on the Internet, you have to know where it is. Sometimes that can be a catch-22. One way to find what you are looking for is to use one of the search engines. In Chapter 2, I provided a short list of search engines. Most browsers include a button labeled "search" that will take you directly to a search engine. You type in the word(s) you are looking for and away it goes. Sometimes it will return a very broad search totally unrelated to your quest, sometimes it will get you right where you want to go. For instance, searching for the word "data" is not going to get you very far.

A natural extension of the *Traders Catalog & Resource Guide* was to put it in electronic form, which I did on the Internet at The Money Mentor (www.moneymentor.com). One of the buttons on the menu will take you directly to a list of all the sources of data of which I am aware. From there you also can find a comparison table of vendors and the type of data they offer. At my office, we scan the Internet daily looking for new resources and link all trading- and investing-related sites to The Money Mentor, our website. (See Figure 3.1.) It's free.

Some of the Internet sites we have found that supply data are listed in Table 3.1.

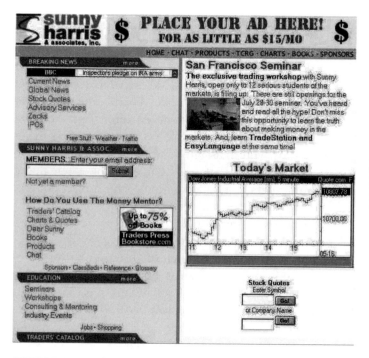

FIGURE 3.1   The Money Mentor (www.moneymentor.com).

Table 3.1 Internet Sources of Data

Big Charts	www.bigcharts.com
CNNfn	www.cnnfn.com/markets/quotes.html
Data Broadcasting Corp.	www.dbc.com
Dial & Chart	www.dialchart.com.au
ESignal	www.esignal.com
Internet Stock Market Resources, Inc.	www.internetstockmarket.com
Money Mentor Quotes	www.moneymentor.com
PCQuote	www.pcquote.com
Quote.com	www.quote.com
StockMaster	www.stockmaster.com
Wall Street City	www.wallstreetcity.com
Yahoo Quotes	www.finance.yahoo.com

Chapter

Analyzing Your Data

CHARTING TECHNIQUES

While technical analysts tend to believe that all the information you need is in price (and sometimes volume), we do not all agree on how to chart prices.

Essentially we use basic geometry to construct a rectangular diagram of price action. A chart consists of a horizontal and a vertical axis, often called the x- and y-axis respectively.

To draw your chart, begin with time as the x-axis and price as the y-axis. Estimate the low and potential highs for the instrument you're following and the time frame you will be observing. The time frame goes on the x-axis, as in Figure 4.1. The price scale goes on the y-axis, as in Figure 4.2. Inevitably, you will use tape or glue, if you are charting by hand, and extend the x- and y-axis of your chart as shown in Figure 4.3. (That is one of the advantages of using a computer. It automatically scales your charts, and you do not run out of room on your paper.)

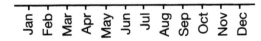

FIGURE 4.1 X-axis showing monthly time frame.

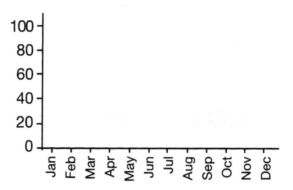

FIGURE 4.2   The vertical y-axis shows price scale.

FIGURE 4.3   Extended chart.

TYPES OF CHARTS

scatter chart
type of chart that shows price occurrences plotted against time.

line chart
type of chart that is similar to the scatter chart but connects the adjacent dots with a straight line.

The simplest chart form, a *scatter chart*, shows a dot at each price occurrence, with the x-axis being time, as in Figure 4.4.

A *line chart* connects adjacent price dots with a straight line, again with time as the x-axis. (See Figure 4.5.)

There is some argument about the validity of connecting the price dots with lines, because no trades actually took place anywhere along that line. The value of drawing the line is the visual clarity it provides you. It is

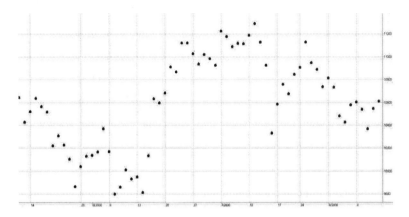

FIGURE 4.4 A scatter chart.

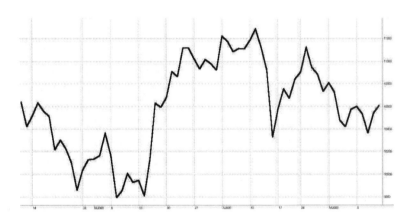

FIGURE 4.5 A line chart.

easier to see direction and patterns with a line chart than with a scatter chart.

A *bar chart* (see Figure 4.6) uses high, low, and closing prices to construct a single bar for each time period.

Each bar represents a single time period, for example, a week, a day, a month, an hour. For that time period—we draw a single vertical line from the highest price to the lowest price that occurred. (See Figure 4.7.)

Then we make a small horizontal mark on the left (the beginning of that time period) showing the price at which that time period opened, and a small horizontal

 bar chart
type of chart constructed out of bars that reflect the price information in a specified time period.

FIGURE 4.6   A bar chart.

mark on the right representing the price at which that period ended. (See Figure 4.8.)

For illustration, let's take a look at the Dow Jones Industrial Average. On June 1, 2000, the DJIA opened at 10,651.80. On June 30, 2000, the DJIA closed at 10,447.80. During June of 2000, the highest price the DJIA ever experienced was 10,862.30 (on June 5, 2000) and the lowest price was 10,335.46 (on June 22, 2000). That information is presented in Figure 4.9.

FIGURE 4.7   A bar showing only high and low.

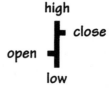

FIGURE 4.8   A bar showing the open, high, low, and close of the period.

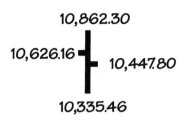

10,862.30

10,626.16 ┤ 10,447.80

10,335.46

FIGURE 4.9 A single monthly bar showing open, high, low, and close.

candlestick charts
charting method, originally from Japan, in which the high and low are plotted as a single line and are referred to as shadows. The price range between the open and the close is plotted as a narrow rectangle and is referred to as the body. If the close is above the open, the body is white. If the close is below the open, the body is black.

A Japanese *candlestick chart* uses the same information as a bar chart, but with an additional piece of information, direction. Figure 4.10 shows how we construct candlestick charts.

A candlestick is a bar—with width and color. The width of each bar is fixed and represents the range between that session's opening and closing. The color of the bar indicates direction.

Later in this chapter we discuss candlestick charting further.

Another chart type that shows open, high, low, and close as well as direction is used by Glenn Neely of the Elliott Wave Institute. Neely's charts show each "bar" as a small chart in itself. While a traditional bar is shown in

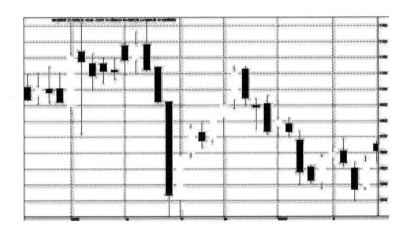

FIGURE 4.10 Japanese candlesticks.

point and figure
type of chart that plots price moves without regard to time. Each column represents a move and continues until the move is reversed and a new column starts.

box
the area of a point-and-figure chart into which the technician places one X or O, representing a given amount of price increase or decrease represented by a box on a point-and-figure chart.

Figure 4.11, a NEoWave bar also shows direction. (See Figure 4.12.)

Point and figure charting was developed by Charles Dow, after whom the Dow Jones Industrial Average and Dow theory have been named. Dow's original charts showed prices and their direction without regard to time. While prices were moving up he wrote the whole dollar price values in a single column, each one on top of the previous price. When prices reversed and began moving down, his chart would move over one column and prices were written below one another in a stack. Original point-and-figure charts looked like the one in Figure 4.13.

This concept was later expanded, using Xs for up moves and Os for down moves and accounting for jerky up-and-down moves, by moving over a column only when price has moved up or down more than a certain amount, called the *box* size.

Point-and-figure charts do not consider time. (See Figure 4.14.) A point-and-figure technician said aptly, "If

FIGURE 4.11 A traditional bar.

FIGURE 4.12 A NEoWave bar.

		47	47
		46	46
45	45	45	45
44	44	44	
43			

FIGURE 4.13 Original point-and-figure charting.

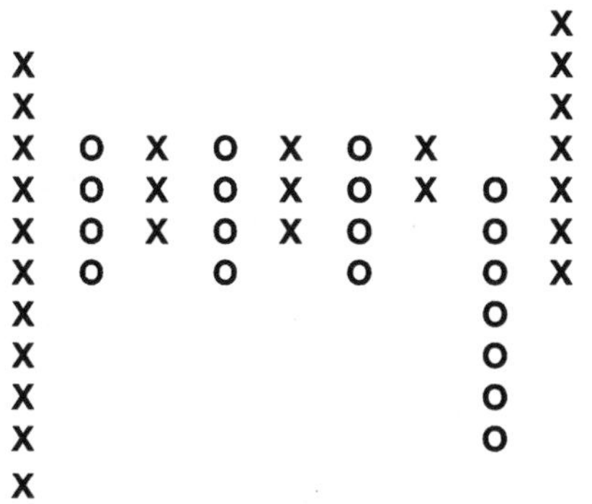

```
                                    X
    X                               X
    X                               X
    X   O   X   O   X   O   X       X
    X   O   X   O   X   O   X   O   X
    X   O   X   O   X   O       O   X
    X   O       O       O       O   X
    X                           O
    X                           O
    X                           O
    X                           O
    X
```

FIGURE 4.14 A point-and-figure chart.

all the information you need is in price, why do you chart time?"

The study of point-and-figure charting includes analytical techniques that are a science in themselves. For in-depth study of this technology, read *Point & Figure Charting* by Thomas J. Dorsey.

TECHNICAL INDICATORS

Most of today's popular technical analysis software comes with a variety of technical indicators preprogrammed for your use. The quotations are built-in; you simply load your chart and click on the indicator you want. The software performs the calculations and displays the chart.

Unless you have some understanding of the theory behind the calculations, you will simply be looking at meaningless squiggles on a computer monitor.

In his book *Technical Analysis from A to Z*, Steven B. Achelis (who is president and founder of Equis, a leading maker of financial software) defines most of the popular indicators, giving an overview, interpretation, and example with each definition. Pick up a copy of *TAAZ* at your local bookstore before you start using any indicators in software packages.

While it may be elegant to have four forks on the left

average directional movement index (ADX)
technical indicator, developed by J. Welles Wilder, that measures a market's trend intensity.

channel
in charting, a price channel contains prices throughout a trend. There are three basic ways to draw channels: parallel, rounded, and those that connect highs or lows.

and three knives and three spoons on the right for a formal meal, one of each will get the job done just as well. Beginners (and even pros) don't need dozens of indicators. All you really need is one good one! Here are a few of the standard technical indicators and their uses.

Average Directional Movement Index (ADX)

For a complete explanation of the *average directional movement index (ADX)* consult *New Concepts in Technical Trading Systems* by J. Welles Wilder, Jr.

ADX is a very powerful tool, as it reveals trends. (See Figure 4.15.) It does not tell you the direction of the trend (use a moving average for that); it just tells you that there is a trend.

Markets trend about 30 percent of the time. That means that markets do not trend about 70 percent of the time. Your studies might lead you to become a trend follower, or they might lead you to trade *channels* in sideways patterns. In either case you had better know which stage the market is in!

The trick with ADX, as with all technical indicators, is to find just the right parameters to use to create a profitable system. Choosing a small number for the length parameter will show you short-term trends, while a large number will show you long-term trends.

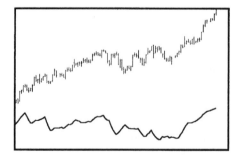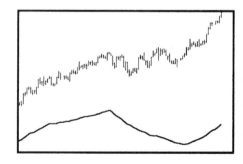

FIGURE 4.15 ADX showing short-term and long-term trends.

Candlesticks

Candlestick charts are older than bar charts and point-and-figure charts but have only recently come into use in the United States. Steve Nison is the acknowledged Western expert on candlestick charting techniques and explains the procedure in *Japanese Candlestick Charting Techniques*.

A candlestick is a bar—with width and color, as in Figure 4.10. The width of each bar is fixed and represents the range between that session's opening and closing. This part of the bar is called the body or real body. The color of the bar indicates direction. If the body is filled (usually black), it means the close was lower than the open—a down bar. An up session is indicated by leaving the body empty, or white. The thin lines above and below the body of the candlestick are called shadows. These lines represent the extremes, the highs and lows of the bar.

Years can be spent trying to understand the basics of candlestick charting and the implications of its many patterns, called revealing names like "hanging man," "dark cloud cover," and "morning star." If this specialty of technical analysis interests you, start with Nison, then read *The Japanese Chart of Charts* by Seiki Shimizu and expand from there.

While many of the popular software packages offer candlestick charting as an indicator, only specialty packages interpret the patterns. The Candlestick Forecaster by International Pacific Trading Company and CandlePower by North Systems all offer candlestick interpretation as well as charting.

Cycles

Cyclical analysis stems from the belief that history repeats itself. The ancients knew about cycles; they documented seasons and lunar cycles, and made calendars. In its simplest form, a financial *cycle* is measured as the distance between successive lows or successive highs in price behavior. (See Figure 4.16.) John F. Ehlers (to my mind the undisputed forerunner of computerized cycle analysis for the markets) in *MESA and Trading Market Cycles* aptly

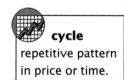
cycle
repetitive pattern in price or time.

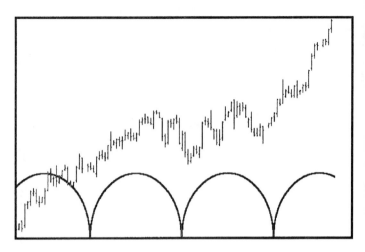

FIGURE 4.16 Simple cycles equidistant from a significant low.

states: "The fact that cycles exist does not imply that they exist all the time. Cycles come and go. External events sometimes dominate and obscure existing cycles. Experience shows that cycles useful for trading are present only about 15 to 30 percent of the time."

Cycles analysis involves the study of overlapping cycles as well as external influences and quickly evolves into harmonic analysis, an esoteric study of the harmony of cycles, astrology, tides, sun spots, and other magnetic forces.

If you become interested in cycles analysis and want to read further, start with *MESA and Trading Market Cycles, Cyclic Analysis in Futures Trading* by Jacob Bernstein, and *The Spiral Calendar* by Christoper Carolan.

You also might want to contact the Foundation for the Study of Cycles, 900 W. Valley Road, Suite 502, Wayne, PA 19087, (610) 995-2120, or at www.cycles.org.

Elliott Wave Theory

R. N. Elliott, the father of the *Elliott Wave Theory*, began formulating his ideas and principles before the crash of 1929, while convalescing from a serious illness. *The Wave Principle* was not published until 1938, and in 1946 he published *Nature's Law—The Secret of the Universe.* Elliott

Elliott Wave Theory pattern recognition technique, published by Ralph N. Elliott in 1939, that holds that the stock market follows a rhythm or pattern of five waves up with three waves down in a bull market and five waves down with three waves up in a bear market to form a complete cycle of eight waves.

believed that his theories were part of the law of the universe, which governs all human activities.

Closely aligned with the work of 13th-century mathematician Leonardo de Pisa, son of Bonaccio (which shortens to Filius Bonacci or Fibonacci), the theory holds that there are repetitive, rhythmical patterns in nature, which in this case form the pattern of five waves up and three waves down, as in Figure 4.17.

In a *bear market* the wave count would be upside down, in other words five waves down and three waves up.

Within each wave is another series of five and three waves, like wooden dolls one inside of another, going on indefinitely, as in Figure 4.18.

The waves have a definite mathematical relationship to each other, based on ratios of Fibonacci numbers, with the ratios 0.618 and 1.618 being dominant factors.

The trick with Elliott wave analysis is to properly recognize the wave count. Elliotticians count the waves as in Figure 4.19.

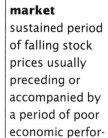

bear market
sustained period of falling stock prices usually preceding or accompanied by a period of poor economic performance known as a recession. The opposite of a bull market.

FIGURE 4.17   Five waves up and three waves down.

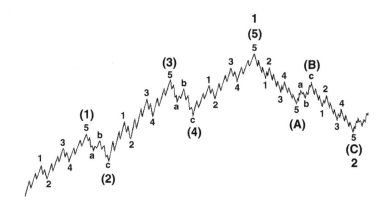

FIGURE 4.18   Waves within waves.

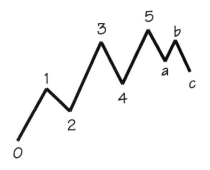

FIGURE 4.19   Counting the waves.

This is one of those IF . . . THEN situations. If you can reliably recognize the 1 wave, or even the 1 and 2 waves, then the theory is predictive—you'll know where the market is headed for the 3, 4, and 5 waves.

Several software products come to mind for Elliott wave analysis: Advanced GET by Trading Techniques, Inc., Bryce Gilmore's Wave Trader, Elliott Wave Systems, Prognosis Software Development's Elwave, Stelar International's Professional Trade Advisor, and WinWaves 32 by Richard Swannell.

Figure 4.20 is a screen capture from Professional Trade Advisor, and shows a sample of the program's ability to run through thousands of calculations to determine the most likely wave count and label the waves accordingly.

An excellent introduction to Elliott wave theory is found in John Murphy's *Technical Analysis of the Futures Markets*. Other books you should study if this theory interests you are: *The Major Works of R. N. Elliott* edited by Robert Prechter; *Elliott Wave Principle* by A. J. Frost and Robert Prechter; and *Fibonacci Applications and Strategies for Traders* by Robert Fischer.

Gann Analysis

W. D. Gann was a legendary stock and commodity trader in the first half of the twentieth century. His work is often mysterious and seemingly based on mathematical and geometric principles combined with astrology and Biblical references.

FIGURE 4.20 Screen capture from Professional Trade Advisor.
(Copyright Stelar International Inc. www.stelaronline.com.)

Gann analysis makes use of important constant angles like 30°, 45°, 60°, and 90° as divisions of the 360° circle as well as squares of numbers, such as 9, 16, and 25. Well known in Gann analysis is the Gann square or Gann wheel from which analysts are able to pinpoint *support* and *resistance* areas with angles drawn from the origin at the center. This square of numbers is formed by placing the beginning price in the center of the square and incrementing clockwise. (See Figure 4.21.)

Analysts then watch the prices on the important angles for support and resistance. (See Figure 4.22.)

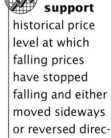

support
historical price level at which falling prices have stopped falling and either moved sideways or reversed direction; usually seen as a price chart pattern.

resistance
price level at
which rising
prices have
stopped rising
and either moved
sideways or re-
versed direction;
usually seen as
a price chart
pattern.

250	255	260	265	270	275	280
245	160	165	170	175	180	285
240	155	110	115	120	185	290
235	150	105	**100**	125	190	295
230	145	140	135	130	195	300
225	220	215	210	205	200	305

FIGURE 4.21 Gann square.

250	255	260	265	270	275	280
245	160	165	170	175	180	285
240	155	110	115	120	185	290
235	150	105	100	125	190	295
230	145	140	135	130	195	300
225	220	215	210	205	200	305

FIGURE 4.22 Gann square with an important angle
marked.

Technical analysis software often provides tools for
drawing Gann angles and squares. With this form of analysis it is important that the size of the squares match the
harmonics of the stock or commodity in question, so don't
just grab the tool and think your analysis is done. Figure
4.23 shows Gann angles and squares as drawn by the computer software, and Figure 4.24 shows a Gann wheel.

This is about as rudimentary as it gets with Gann
analysis, which is a very complex field requiring years of
study. For a clear and concise introduction to the concepts, see James Hyerczyk's *Pattern Price and Time*. If you
are interested in delving further, a subscription to *Traders'
World* magazine is in order. This quarterly publication explores Gann and Elliott work as well as astrological analysis and is available from Larry Jacobs at Halliker's Inc.

Much of Gann's original and reprinted work is
maintained by Nikki Jones of Lambert-Gann Publishing.
One of Gann's more fascinating works is *Tunnel Thru the
Air or Looking Back from 1940*, which he wrote in 1927.
Many of the events, inventions, and market panics and

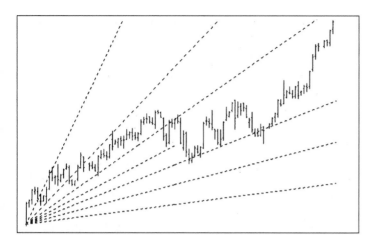

FIGURE 4.23 Gann fann generated by software.

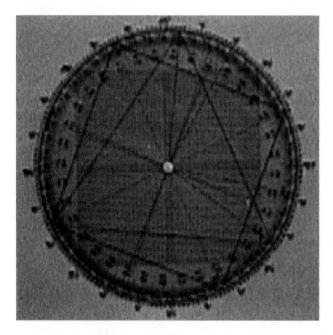

FIGURE 4.24 Gann wheel.

booms mentioned in the book actually came about in later years. In the foreword Gann confidently states: "This story is founded on facts and events . . . which will happen in the future."

MACD

MACD (moving average convergence-divergence) difference between two exponentially smoothed moving averages of different length (often 12 and 24 period). Technicians often use the crossing of this value over the zero line to signal buying or selling opportunities.

Introduced in 1979 by Gerald Appel, *MACD* stands for moving average convergence-divergence. The original 20-page pamphlet, "The Moving Average Convergence-Divergence Trading Method—Advanced Version," by Gerald Appel, explains his calculations and methodology.

Most popular software sets the default values for the MACD at 12, 26, 9 for the first and second exponential averages and the period of the exponential average of the difference, respectively. Experimentation with these numbers is in order because different markets follow different periodicities. Study the examples of the S&P 500 index in Figure 4.25, one with the values of the MACD set at the default 12, 26, 9 and the second with the values set much closer together at 9, 13, 7.

The crossover points on the second MACD occur sooner, potentially giving earlier market timing signals.

In *Short-Term Trading in Futures*, Jake Bernstein em-

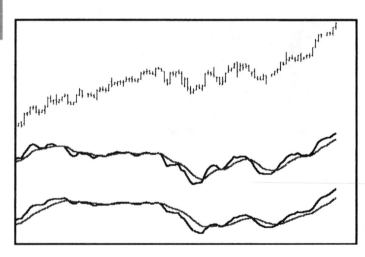

FIGURE 4.25 MACD 12, 26, 9 and MACD 9, 13, 7.

ploys MACD, which he calls DEMA (dual exponential moving averages), in excellent examples of trading systems. I highly recommend this book as a quick-start for all traders, not just futures traders.

Remember that technical analysis and charting methods are of general application, and don't be frightened just because a book has the word "futures" in the title.

McClellan Oscillator

The popular McClellan oscillator is an interpretation of the advance-decline line developed by Sherman and Marian McClellan, which measures the short-term overbought/oversold condition of the market as a whole, using the NYSE as proxy. (See Figure 4.26.)

The companion indicator, the McClellan summation index, shows the intermediate-to-long-term direction of the market—up or down. These two indicators are relatively straightforward and a great place to start your analysis and research.

For further reading, the definitive work on these indicators is by the McClellans themselves in *Patterns for Profit*. Another source for how-to, as well as current interpretation of the McClellans' work, is Kennedy Gammage of The Richland Company. Gammage authored *The Special Orientation Report*, which does an admirable job of summarizing the construction and use of the oscillator and summation index.

Momentum

Webster defines *momentum* as "the impetus of a moving object." That definition gives me a better mental picture of its use in the markets than the standard used by technical analysts, where momentum is the velocity of price change over the momentum period. $M = C_0 - C_i$ where C_0 is the current closing price and C_i is the closing price i time periods ago.

Steven Achelis in *Technical Analysis from A to Z* defines momentum as a measure of "the amount that a security's price has changed over a given time span."

momentum
time series representing change of today's price from some fixed number of days back in history.

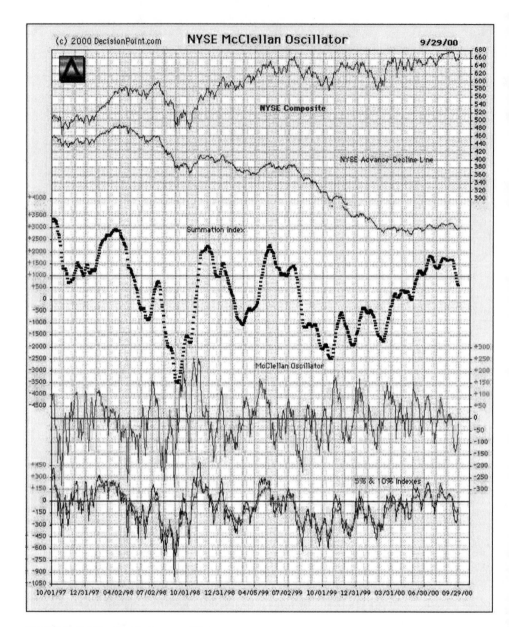

FIGURE 4.26 McClellan oscillator.
(Chart courtesy of www.decisionpoint.com.)

Observation of momentum will tell you the speed of the market. I look at momentum as a measure of rate of change, which tells me how many dollars per hour a security moves. There is only one reason to trade: to make money. Given that as your premise, you'd better know how much money potential there is in a given instrument. Interpretation of momentum is where you find that answer.

Moving Averages

A moving average is a way to smooth the noise in data so that the trend is easier to see. (See Figure 4.27.)

Mathematically a simple moving average is the sum of a value plus a selected number of previous values divided by the total number of values.

simple moving average $= [V_1 + V_2 + \ldots + V_n]/n$

Moving averages can be simple, weighted, or exponential. This equation calculates a simple moving average, the total of values divided by the number of values. This type of averaging gives equal weight to each day's values.

What if the characteristics of the market are chang-

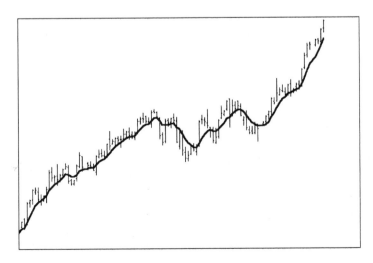

FIGURE 4.27 Simple moving average.

ing, so that the data closer to now are more important than the data from a long time ago? A weighted moving average gives more importance to the more recent values by use of multipliers (weighting factors.) (See Figure 4.28.) The farthest value is multiplied by 1, the second value by 2, and so on until coming to the most recent data. For instance, with five data values, the first is multiplied by 1, the second by 2, the third by 3, the fourth by 4, and the fifth by 5. Then the sum of all these products is divided by the sum of the multipliers (1 + 1 + 3 + 4 + 5 = 15 in this case).

$$\text{WMAV} = \frac{\{\,[n - (n - 1)\,]*V_2 + \ldots + n*V_n\,\}}{\{\,n + (n - 1) + (n - 2) + \ldots + [n - (n - 1)]\,\}}$$

The weighted moving average weights the recent data more heavily than older data. Still, both this and the simple moving average only take into account the data in the specific time frame, or window of time.

To take into account all the known data for a security or contract, we would use an *exponential moving average* (cmav), which begins with the first value and accumulates the data while it gives more weight to the more recent data. This is not a calculation you will want

> **exponential moving average (EMA)**
> EMA for day i is calculated as:
> $A_i = \alpha P_i + (1 - \alpha)(A_{i-1})$, where P is the price on day i and α (alpha) is a smoothing constant ($0 < \alpha < i$). Alpha may be estimated as $2/(n + 1)$, where n is the length of the simple moving average.

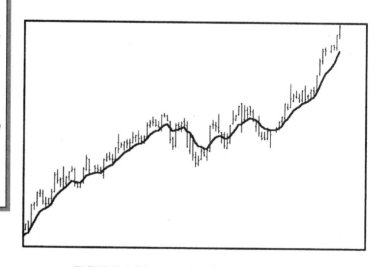

FIGURE 4.28 Weighted moving average.

to run by hand, so don't plan on using exponential moving averages without a computer. For my trading, I use exponential moving averages that I have "tweaked" mathematically, but they are still moving averages. (See Figure 4.29.)

EMAVs seem to give more timely signals, especially in faster markets.

$$A_i = \alpha P_i + (1 - \alpha)A_{i-1}$$

where P is the price on day i and α (alpha) is a smoothing constant $(0<\alpha<1)$. Alpha may be estimated as $2/(n + 1)$, where n is the simple moving average length.

Most of the popular technical analysis software products have all three of these moving average types available as indicators, so you don't have to calculate anything; you just click on the chart and click on the indicator you want.

Pattern Recognition

Pattern recognition is a matter of repeatedly asking the question "What is true here?" Probably the most prolific

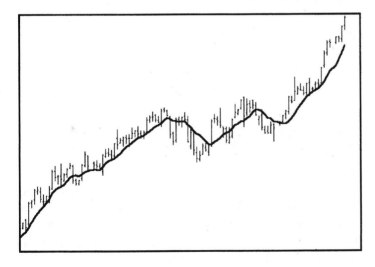

FIGURE 4.29 Exponential moving average.

pattern recognizer in this business is Larry Williams, whose books *The Definitive Guide to Futures Trading* and *The Definitive Guide to Futures Trading Volume II* can give you a good foundation in the process of recognizing patterns.

Williams is an ace at recognizing patterns in the market and then applying statistical analysis to get an idea of how often this pattern occurs and the likelihood of making a winning trade when you see the pattern again.

Pattern recognition is kind of like one of those word puzzles for kids, where you are to circle all the words you see:

A	V	C	Y	C	L	E
Q	O	Z	U	A	O	A
B	L	A	C	K	X	R
M	U	D	P	I	E	T
X	M	Y	W	A	N	H
E	E	L	M	A	V	S

Rather than trying to decipher a jumble of letters, you are analyzing a jumble of numbers or visually inspecting patterns in charts.

For instance, in *The Definitive Guide to Futures Trading Volume II*, Williams notes that: "If we have 3 consecutive down closes in the S&P, you have a 64.6 percent probability of an up day tomorrow."

The pattern is three consecutive down closes followed by an up day. The statistical analysis tells you how likely the pattern is to happen.

TRADING SOFTWARE

Hundreds of software products will produce charts for traders. The obvious advantage to using software is speed. The drawback to using software, especially in the beginning of your training, is that you don't get a "feel" for the market you are studying as you do when you create all your charts by hand.

When racing sports cars, you first look at the track, then walk the track several times, then drive the track slowly before considering actually driving with any speed. Walking the track allows your body's memory to incorporate distance and curves into its neurology.

If you begin your trading career by making all your charts by hand, your neurology will suggest theories for trading systems later on when you do your research. Something happens in your subconscious when you draw one bar at a time over a long time frame, which reveals itself later as "intuition."

Therefore, even if all your trading and research is going to be computerized, start by making your charts with pencil and paper. After your subconscious is attuned to the market, you can begin to work with computerized charts. If you begin with computer-generated charts, you'll find that you miss the nuances of the market and can't quite ever seem to find a system that really works.

As in televised cooking shows where they mix up the batter and then take a finished cake out of the oven, let's skip to the point in time where you are intimately familiar with the markets you have been studying. That could be in several months or in several years. By that time you will know what type of charting interests you and can intelligently select software to perform the charting function.

What software will not do is generate ideas. You must hold brainstorming sessions. Customarily brainstorming sessions are conducted in a room with a white board and markers, a person who acts not as moderator but as clerk to write down the ideas, and all the people involved in a project. A question is brought under consideration and everyone speaks freely as ideas come to mind.

As a trader you will have brainstorming sessions with yourself. Write down all possible research avenues as they occur to you. I always keep a small six-ring binder with me in which to write these notes. You never know when ideas will pop to the surface.

ANALYSIS PROCESS

What's the goal here? Without a specific goal, you are not going to achieve one.

Goals like "I wanna be rich" are not specific. Trading is not an easy field in which to become rich. In fact, trading is not an easy field in which even to make a living. The easy part is to lose all your trading capital and give up.

In the analysis process you are going to look at thousands of charts and ask yourself "What is true here?" You are working a complicated logic problem. Here is where your brainstorming comes in. Let's look at the chart in Figure 4.30 and brainstorm together.

Now, let's begin to ask "What is true here?" It is true that the market (it does not matter what market this is) moves sharply upward in the beginning, then moves sideways for most of the chart, and toward the end moves sharply upward again. It is true that there are several smaller moves within the large moves. It is true that some of the bars in this chart seem to show *volatility*, that is, the range (the distance between the high and low) appears large compared to some of the other bars in this chart.

Before applying any indicators or trend lines to this chart, I always ask whether it is worth my time. This is

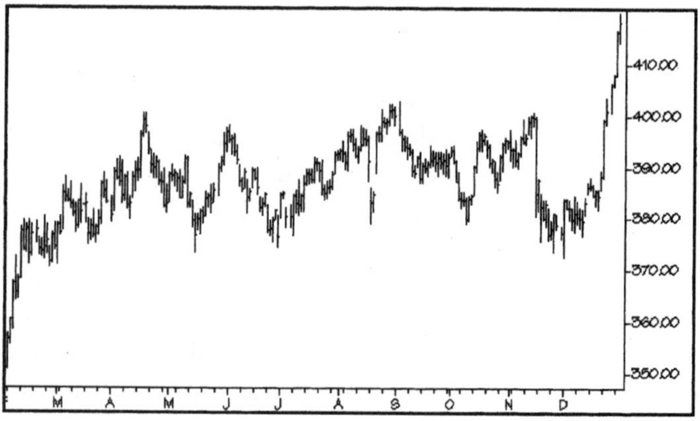

volatility measure of the degree of stability of the price of a stock, index, or commodity. A highly volatile stock, one that experiences wide price swings, is considered to be more speculative than one with a low volatility.

FIGURE 4.30 Brainstorm with this chart.

your job and you need to be paid a decent hourly wage. What hourly wage will this market allow? How do you figure that out?

First, let's mark the obvious highs and lows on the chart in Figure 4.31. We will use up-triangles to denote a low (from which the market moves up) and a down-triangle to denote a high (from which the market moves down).

We don't know yet whether there is any money to be made here; we have just marked potential entry points and exit points.

Next we need to look at the scale of this chart to see whether the market movements between our entries and exits would be profitable. If, for instance, the time frame of this chart were a year and each move would give us only a couple of dollars profit, it is not worth our time. But if it is a year and each move produces thousands of dollars, we will go further with our analysis.

The scale on the right side of the chart shows that the data move from 350 to 410, a 60-point move. This chart happens to be of the S&P 500 index (my favorite trading vehicle), but it doesn't matter what we are observing, the test for fitness is the same. In the S&P 500, a move of one point is worth $250 so a move from 1350 to 1410 would be worth 60 × $250. The time frame in question is from February through December, a period of 11

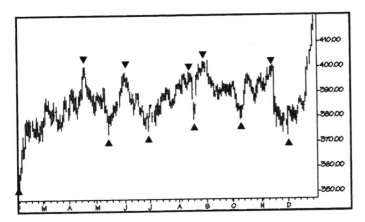

FIGURE 4.31 Mark potential entries and exits.

months. Fifteen thousand dollars in 11 months, that's $1,250 per month or $7.25 per hour. That is our first rough approximation.

Next we will pretend that we could catch each trade we have marked correctly at the precise highs and lows. We will calculate each trade's profit or loss and see what hourly wage could have been produced. The trades are displayed in Figure 4.32.

reversal system
system in which each signal closes the previous position and opens another, opposite position.

This type of trading system is called a *reversal system*. You are always in the market, either long or short. Note that we have used closing prices for all the trades. The assumption here is that we have bought or sold the market at the closing price of the day, not any of the intraday prices.

Calculating our potential hourly wage, we find that $147,500 in 11 months is $13,400 per month, or $80 per hour assuming a 40-hour work week. That is respectable.

Now for a moment of truth. Before we can go any further, we must take a second look at our pretense of catching each market move at the top and the bottom. That will never happen. As a rule of thumb, I make the assumption that a good system can catch 40-60 percent of each market move. That is pretty realistic. With this in

trade nbr	type	date	entry	date	exit	profit/loss
1	buy	1-Feb	350	25-Apr	400	$25,000
2	sell	25-Apr	400	10-May	375	$12,500
3	buy	10-May	375	1-Jun	400	$12,500
4	sell	1-Jun	400	1-Jul	375	$12,500
5	buy	1-Jul	375	12-Aug	400	$12,500
6	sell	12-Aug	400	16-Aug	380	$10,000
7	buy	16-Aug	380	1-Sep	400	$10,000
8	sell	1-Sep	400	10-Oct	380	$10,000
9	buy	10-Oct	380	4-Nov	400	$10,000
10	sell	4-Nov	400	1-Dec	375	$12,500
11	buy	1-Dec	375	31-Dec	415	$20,000
					TOTAL	$147,500

FIGURE 4.32 Trading log of potential entries and exits.

mind, 50 percent of $147,500 is $73,750 which, using 2,000 hours per year as a quick estimate, gives us $36.88 per hour trading one contract.

I call this part of the data analysis the "potential hourly wage analysis," or PHW. Before jumping into the numerical or pattern analysis phase, it is important to conduct these calculations. If the hourly wage is not acceptable, why would you want to spend time conducting all the remaining research?

DIGITAL VERSUS ANALOG ANALYSIS

In the early days of computer technology, there was great debate about whether the digital or the analog computer would win over the marketplace. Likewise, there is debate among technical analysts about whether the answers to the market's movement lie in digital or analog analysis.

What's the difference? Digital analysis is discrete; that is, each point of analysis is separate and distinct from the next. Digital analysis looks like a scatter chart. (See Figure 4.33.)

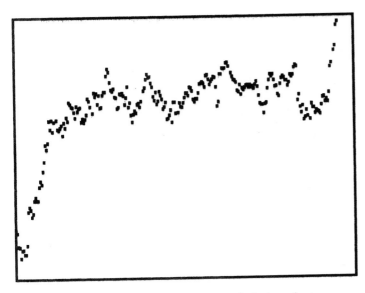

FIGURE 4.33 Discrete points; digital analysis.

On the other hand, analog analysis is continuous, whether the data are or not. Analog analysis looks like an average of the connected points. (See Figure 4.34.) Analog analysis interpolates between points, creating data where there are none. Digital analysis assumes that patterns repeat themselves.

NUMERICAL ANALYSIS

Numerical analysis is the process of finding equations that describe the movement we observe in the market.

trend line
straight line on a chart that shows the market's direction.

Numerical analysis can be as simple as drawing a straight line showing the market's direction. That's called a *trend line*. Or it can be as complex as multiple sets of nonlinear equations or neural networks. Most of the technical indicators described earlier in this chapter are numerical in nature, as are most technical indicators.

How do we use numerical analysis? Let's look back to the chart with the up- and down-arrows. (See Figure 4.31.) That chart exhibits the ideal system: It catches all the highs and lows. Our goal, then, is to get as close to this as we can with equations. We'll begin our search with

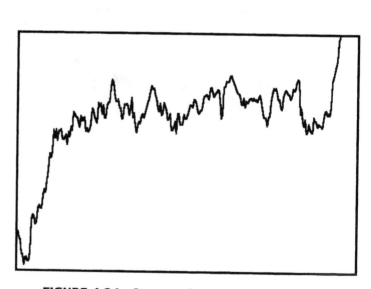

FIGURE 4.34 Connected points; analog analysis.

moving averages. In Chapter 15 we will go into the process in depth.

With technical analysis software (i.e., MetaStock, TradeStation, SuperCharts, SMARTrader, Pattern Smasher, QCharts, eSignal, TeleChart 2000, I overlay an 18-period moving average on the chart. (See Figure 4.35.)

On inspection I see that this moving average is too slow. It does not turn as fast as the market turns. After some experimentation with input values, I find that a five-period moving average looks pretty good. (See Figure 4.36.)

Numerical analysis can take this form, where we use a prepackaged computer program to overlay indicators and test ideas, or it can become as complicated as writing your own programs to analyze the raw data. That process is well beyond the scope of this book, however.

PATTERN ANALYSIS

Pattern recognition is the process of finding recurring patterns in the market movement we observe.

As you repeatedly ask the question "What is true?",

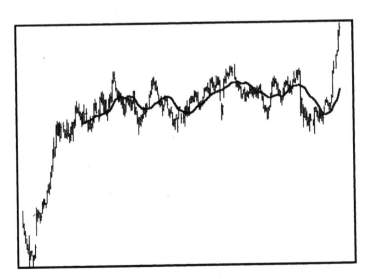

FIGURE 4.35 18-period moving average.

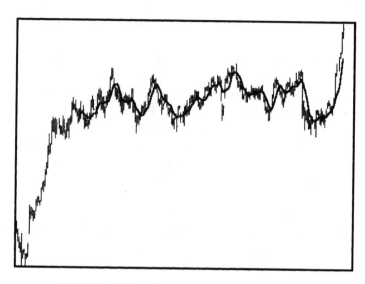

FIGURE 4.36 Five-period moving average.

you are looking for profitable market moves in an attempt to decipher what went before.

If you can observe many profitable moves that all occur after a common event, you may have found a pattern. The only way to know for sure is through diligent testing of hundreds of observations.

Here, for instance, is an example of a pattern Williams revealed at a recent meeting of technical analysts: "The pattern is set up when there is a day whose low is the lowest low of the last four days and has a down close. If the close two days after this low-range day is greater than the low day's high, buy on the close."

A pictorial representation of the pattern is shown in Figure 4.37.

FIGURE 4.37 A typical Larry Williams pattern setup.

Pattern analysis is in many ways more difficult than numerical analysis, because you cannot just throw a computer program on it and crunch away. Look at its intricacies. The pattern in Figure 4.37 is a small section of a much larger chart. Would you have seen that pattern in a forest full of bars? If this type of analysis interests you, Larry Williams can be reached at CTI Publishing, (800) 800-8333.

Exploring the Literature

Hundreds of books have been written about financial matters, with topics ranging from *Advanced Commodity Trading Techniques* to *Zen in the Markets*. It's difficult to read them all, so let's first look at a few which I believe are on the "required reading" list for new traders.

CONTRARY INVESTING— THE INSIDER'S GUIDE TO BUYING LOW AND SELLING HIGH by Richard E. Band

Richard Band, editor of *Personal Finance*, publishes one of the nation's most widely read investment newsletters. His market forecasts have been quoted in *Business Week*, *USA Today*, and other national publications, and he has appeared on CBS News and the Public Broadcasting Service.

In this book Band presents simple, sane, and reliable techniques for contrary investing. He lists signs of impending market reversals, a stock trading system, a contrarian approach to investing in mutual funds, and ways to spot tops and bottoms in the real estate market.

ECONOMICS—A SELF-TEACHING GUIDE by Stephen L. Slavin

A sound foundation in the theory of economics will serve you well in your preparation for trading. Understanding what others think moves the economy will give you a foundation from which you can begin to question the standard principles and begin to form your own.

Economics—A Self-Teaching Guide is probably the easiest to handle and yet most thorough guide you can find to lead you through this process. Beginning with a short history lesson and moving right into a review of the mathematics and charting techniques you will need, this book covers supply and demand, gross national product, consumption, inflation, unemployment, fiscal policy, and the Federal Reserve in a way that makes it all seem easy.

At the end of each chapter is a short test, with answers, to help you review the preceding material. This step-by-step, self-paced format makes the learning process fun.

A SHORT HISTORY OF FINANCIAL EUPHORIA by John Kenneth Galbraith

John Kenneth Galbraith is Professor of Economics Emeritus at Harvard University and was the U.S. Ambassador to India during the Kennedy administration. His works include *The Great Crash 1929, The Affluent Society, The New Industrial State*, and *Economics and the Public Purpose*.

A mere 113-page pocket book, *A Short History of Financial Euphoria* will do more to enlighten you about the nature of the markets than any other book of which I am aware. Entertaining and educational, this book will show you why the market not only has but will continue to have periods of boom and bust.

THE INTELLIGENT INVESTOR
by Benjamin Graham

Former president of the Graham-Newman Corporation
and Columbia University Graduate School of Business
teacher, Benjamin Graham provides a conservative and
safe approach to investing, making a strong case for stock
investment strategies.

KEYS TO UNDERSTANDING
THE FINANCIAL NEWS
by Nick Apostolou and
D. Lawrence Cumbley

One of the Barron's Business Keys series, this little pocket
book is packed with quick-reference explanations of leading economic indicators, the Federal Reserve system,
money supply, interest rates, productivity, stock, over-the-
counter market, mutual funds, advisory services, municipal bonds, futures, corporate information, and mergers
and acquisitions.

    Keys to Understanding the Financial News gives you
a shortcut to mastering key concepts and financial terminology.

MONEY GUIDE: THE STOCK MARKET

The editors of *Money* magazine have put together a clear,
concise guide with strategies and tactics for surviving on
Wall Street. I don't buy their claim that it can "be the avenue to Easy Street," but I do believe they do a good job of
summarizing the process.

    Covering initial public offerings, over-the-counter
stocks, Value Line, Standard & Poor's, annual reports,
takeovers and turnarounds, options, foreign stocks, and
margin accounts, this little book will give you a good
foundation in the essentials of stock trading.

OPTIONS AS A STRATEGIC INVESTMENT—A COMPREHENSIVE ANALYSIS OF LISTED OPTION STRATEGIES by Lawrence G. McMillan

This one's a toughie. Even though it is difficult reading, it is *the* book to read on options. Formatted like a college math or physics text, this encyclopedia of options trading is a full semester's work. Every equation, all the explanations, and all the examples you could ever ask for will give you the complete course on trading options.

STRATEGIC INVESTMENT TIMING by Dick A. Stoken

Strategic Investment Timing is loaded with information. If you have ever wondered if there is a right time to invest in real estate and a right time to invest in bonds and another right time for stocks, this book will answer all your questions.

With historical examples and statistics, Stoken builds his case for market timing. He tells you where to find the numbers you will need to track market activity and measure the investment climate. You will even learn how to predict presidential elections and what to invest in during both inflationary and deflationary times.

TECHNICAL ANALYSIS OF THE FUTURES MARKETS: A COMPREHENSIVE GUIDE TO TRADING METHODS AND APPLICATIONS by John J. Murphy

This is the one book that I believe you must memorize. I did. Of the many books on technical analysis, this one is at the same time the most comprehensive and the easiest to understand. It does not just give you a list of indicators and their equations; it gives you all the explanations and examples you need to understand them. I have two copies of this book, one of which is completely worn out.

TECHNICAL ANALYSIS
FROM A TO Z by Steven B. Achelis

President and founder of Equis International, a leading maker of financial software, Steven Achelis has provided a clear and concise guide to technical indicators. Achelis explores 100 indicators, giving an overview, interpretation, and example of each. Where applicable, he provides equations and calculation methods.

THE ULTIMATE MUTUAL
FUND GUIDE by Warren Boroson

Mutual fund timing and switching is perhaps the best initial entry to trading. It is certainly less risky than options or futures, and you can begin your education with a relatively small outlay of capital.

If you are considering this approach, you need a solid foundation in the overall theory of mutual funds. *The Ultimate Mutual Fund Guide* is the synthesis of the author's poll of 17 mutual fund authorities, giving you a comprehensive analysis of the experts' choices for best funds.

WALL STREET JOURNAL GUIDE TO
UNDERSTANDING MONEY & MARKETS

Shaped rather like a travel guide, this 120-page book consists of pictures with explanations. It covers the basics of stocks, bonds, mutual funds, futures, options, and money. If you are just starting out, the *Wall Street Journal Guide* will give you all the answers to those questions you are embarrassed to ask the professionals.

UPWARD AND ONWARD

The books listed constitute your beginning study list. Once you completely understand each of those books, you can move on to books that explore these topics in greater detail, and you can begin to study some of the fun stuff. The fun stuff includes proclamations of outrageous success, books that purport to reveal trading systems, and tales of inside, true-life experience.

Don't start with the fun stuff. If you do, you will get the mistaken impression that trading is loads of excitement, easy riches, and being in the right place at the right time. It is not. Trading is a lot of hard work, study, and research, followed by a lot of hard work, concentration, and discipline.

An extended book list is provided in the Bibliography, alphabetical by author. This list does not tell you what to read next, but it will give you an idea of the volume of material that is available to you. Probably the best idea at this point is for you to go to www.moneymentor.com and click on [Books]. There I have links to financial booksellers, where you can browse to your heart's content.

Clubs and Professional Organizations

NETWORKING

The synergy between people working in groups sparks creativity. For this reason it is a good idea to find a group or groups in your area that are interested in trading and investing. Often local computer users groups have financial subinterest groups. And frequently groups that have the word "investing" in their title are more interested in speculating and trading.

The American Association of Individual Investors (AAII), a nonprofit educational organization, holds regular meetings in most cities. Find a group in your area, and attend meetings during your learning phase. By so doing, you also will connect with other groups and glean ideas you would otherwise not find.

The Market Technician's Association, with headquarters in New York, has local chapters in many larger cities. Often these chapters hold monthly or quarterly meetings to which the public is welcome.

Most software vendors have users' groups that meet locally. Among those offering regular meetings are the Fast Track Users Group, MetStock Users Group, and

SuperCharts Users Group. In Appendix C you'll find numbers for software vendors; they'll be happy to hear from you. The Money Mentor provides a calendar of users' group meetings and locations (www.moneymentor. com). Just click on [Index] and then [U] for Users' Groups.

DON'T GET STUCK

While networking and sharing ideas is important in the beginning phases of trading and investing, for some people it becomes not the means but the end in itself. Don't confuse attending meetings with trading. At some point, you must develop your own theories, test them, and begin to trade.

GUIDE TO MEETINGS

I cannot possibly provide you with a complete list of all the various meetings, clubs, and other organizations in this book. At my office, we try to keep our Internet site, The Money Mentor, up to date with times, places, and topics for upcoming meetings. Look to it for these particulars, or if you have information to share, we will put it on the Internet for free. Under [Users' Groups] in the index you will find locations and times of meetings for various groups.

USERS' GROUPS

Most of the major software vendors sponsor users' groups, which are local groups of people who meet at a certain time and place to compare experiences with that software and share techniques and views on the market. Not only valuable for current users of the software, these meetings are a great way to meet people who can tell you about their satisfaction (or lack thereof) with the software product and with whom you share a common interest—trading. Often these groups have notable guest speakers, who can add to your techniques and learning experience. Call the contact person listed in The Money Mentor for information about upcoming meetings; often the times and places vary depending on holidays and speaker availability.

Chapter 7

Evaluating Seminars and Conferences

To me a seminar, conference, or workshop is worth the attendance fee if I get one solid idea from it that improves my trading.

If you are looking for boondoggle seminars where you can write off your play time you are in the wrong business and have come to the wrong source. Don't get me wrong, I like my play time too. But not at the expense of my trading.

As in any profession, once you get on one mailing list, you will be on them all. When that happens you will begin to receive mailings about every conceivable get-rich-quick scheme as well as every work-your-tail-off-and-learn-something seminar and conference. You cannot go to them all. It is your job to sort through them to find the ones that will benefit you most.

If you have the time and the money, I suggest you start by going to one of the get-rich-quick seminars. You will see what they are all about and, it is hoped, get it over with. We are all tempted to believe that someone else has the answer and that this process is easier than we are finding it to be. The lure of instant riches is seductive.

Once you get that out of your system, it is time to start going to serious seminars that will feed you as much information as you can handle. You need to learn as much as you possibly can.

Many of the software vendors offer relatively inexpensive seminars designed to teach you about their software specifically and about trading techniques in general. Try OptionVue Systems International (800) 733-6610 and Omega Research (305) 485-7000; both offer educational seminars. Call to ask for a schedule of upcoming seminars.

Futures magazine sponsors the Futures Expo, which is independent of any particular software vendor and general in nature, bringing you the latest speakers and their techniques (see www.futuresmag.com). They can be reached at (800) 221-4352.

By far the best seminar for beginning traders, the TAG Seminars, is not sponsored by a software vendor but is independently sponsored by Ino.com. The seminar is usually held in the fall. While this is not meant to be an advertisement for their sessions, TAG does a fantastic job of enlisting speakers from the trading community who are at the leading edge of their fields. The speakers are not employed by TAG but are brought in just for these talks, which take place over three days. Each year the seminar brings new speakers so it is wise to attend year after year to stay on top of the latest in techniques and technologies. The three days of learning are intense and challenging as well as fun. Conference organizers can be reached at (888) TAG-0858.

Throughout the year seminars and conferences are sponsored by a variety of organizations, each devoted to different aspects of trading. The content of most of these seminars is not directed to beginners, however. Nevertheless, it is important that you know about these seminars as you set your long-range goals:

American Management Association (800) 262-9699
Blanchard & Co., Inc. (800) 880-4653
FIA—Futures Industry Association (202) 466-5460
FOW—Futures and Options World 001-071+827-9977
ISI—Investment Seminars Inc. (800) 226-0323
MAR—Managed Account Reports (212) 213-6202

MFA—Managed Futures Association (415) 325-3133
Morningstar (312) 696-6000
MTA—Market Technicians Association (212) 912-0995
NYMEX—New York Mercantile Exchange
    (212) 938-2222
Risk Management Conferences (800) OPTIONS

In addition, many exchanges offer seminars and workshops that are educational in nature. Contact their public relations department or their library for specific information:

CBOE—Chicago Board Options Exchange
    (800) OPTIONS
CBOT—Chicago Board of Trade (800) THE-CBOT
CME—Chicago Mercantile Exchange (312) 930-8236
LIFFE—London International Financial Futures &
    Options Exhange (212) 385-1515
NYFE—New York Futures Exchange (800) 843-6933

Check the Nasdaq-Amex web site at www.nasdaq.com for information about their seminars.

Chapter

Charlatans and
Their Techniques

While it is not necessary to devote very much space to this topic, it must be addressed briefly. In all endeavors involving the exchange of money, there is always someone who wants a free lunch and is willing to cheat to get it. Standing in the bushes is Little Red Riding Hood's wolf, ready to take advantage of the unsuspecting.

In your analysis of any purchase, keep in mind that anything that seems too good to be true probably is. If you are looking for a free lunch, you will probably get it handed to you on a plate.

Trading is a difficult business that takes many years to learn and many failures to teach you the lessons. You cannot expect to step up to the plate for the first time and hit a home run.

Be suspicious of advertisements that guarantee you thousands of percent profit for no work on your part. Be wary of vendors who promise you instant success. Do your homework before you purchase any software, newsletter, fax service, trading system, or seminar.

Some time ago a subscriber of my magazine, *Traders' Catalog & Resource Guide*, called to say that he would be willing to pay $10,000 for every trading system he could

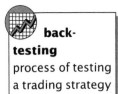

back-testing

process of testing a trading strategy on historical data.

find that was profitable. His only condition was that he be given the system in password-protected computer code, so that he could conduct the *back-testing* himself. This caller wanted to place a classified ad to this effect in the upcoming issue of the guide. I told him I would not take the ad and, further, warned him that he could lose a lot of money on this venture. Unconvinced, he wanted to know how this was possible, since he would be personally conducting the testing.

Creating a system that works in the past is very simple. Creating a system that works in the future is an enormous project indeed. But he didn't ask for a system that works in the future. I explained to this caller that I could simply take the known data for the S&P 500 index from 1982 to the present and pick all the highs and lows, create a database of the dates of those important price points, and generate trades based on those specific dates. Protecting the "system" with a password and selling it to him to test would generate outstanding results. But it would never work for any future trade, and he would be out $10,000.

Since I thought of that little "sure-thing" system off the top of my head, I can only assume that clever people out there can generate many more schemes to liberate you from your cash.

DON'T LET THE GOBLINS GET YOU

There are several ways to locate information about products or services in which you are interested, sort of like a *Consumer Reports* for traders. Several companies have established their businesses around tracking the performance of other peoples' businesses.

If you are considering the purchase of a trading system, call John Hill at Futures Truth, where they test publicly offered trading systems and rank their performance. For a small fee ($35 at the time of this printing) you can purchase the latest ranking information reporting on more than 150 systems, which could save you from tremendous losses.

John Hill
Futures Truth
815 Hillside Road
Hendersonville, NC 28739
(704) 697-0273   fax (704) 692-7375

Another source of valuable information is Club 3000, where Bo Thunman publishes, in newsletter format, the compilation of commentary from users all over the world who are offering their insights and comments about vendors and systems with which they have experience.

Bo Thunman
Club 3000
4550 N 38th Street
Augusta, MI 49012
(616) 731-5600   fax (616) 731-5600

If you are considering subscribing to an advisory newsletter, you might want to know the author's track record before you do so. For nearly 20 years Mark Hulbert has followed the performance of the recommendations collected in 400 portfolios. And he gives you objective performance figures in his publication.

Mark Hulbert
Hulbert Financial Digest
316 Commerce Street
Alexandria, VA 22314
(888) HULBERT   fax (703) 836-5866
www.hulbertdigest.com

Looking for a professional money manager? Before completing the transaction, check the following sources for statistics on the traders you are considering:

The Barclay Institutional Report
Sol Waksman
Barclay Trading Group, Ltd.
508 N 2nd Street, Suite 201
Fairfield, IA 52556-2464
(800) 338-2827   fax (515) 472-9514

Quarterly Performance Report
Lois Peltz
MAR—Managed Account Reports
220 Fifth Avenue, 19th Floor
New York, NY 10001
(212) 213-6202   fax (212) 213-1870
www.marhedge.com

Looking for just the right mutual fund? Consult first with:

Morningstar Mutual Funds
Morningstar, Inc.
225 West Wacker Drive
Chicago, IL 60606
(800) 876-5005   fax (312) 696-6001
www.morningstar.com

And then you can do comparison shopping.

If it is stocks that you are looking for, do your comparison shopping with the ultimate research tool:

Value Line Investment Survey
Value Line
71 Third Avenue
New York, NY 10017-4064
(800) 634-3583   fax (212) 338-9623
www.valueline.com

Above all, do not get caught unprepared. Do your homework before you buy.

FURTHER READING

Where Are the Customers' Yachts? by Fred Schwed, Jr.
Den of Thieves by James B. Stewart

What Do You Trade?

D o not buy something you cannot sell.
Before trading anything, you need to be certain that there is a liquid market for it. Your condominium may be worth jillions on paper, but if you cannot get rid of it, it is really worth nothing.

Look at the volume and number of shares of a stock being traded before you jump in. If it is futures you are trading, first consult the "Trading Liquidity" table in each issue of *Technical Analysis of Stocks and Commodities* magazine. If the liquidity is high, you will be able to get in and out of your trades; if not, you might get stuck.

TRADING VEHICLES

Bonds

Bonds are simply loans that you are making to someone else: Government bonds, corporate bonds, and municipal bonds are examples. The certificate for that bond shows the interest rate you are being paid, the maturity of the loan, and the par value (the amount you will be paid when the loan is over). The bond certificate is negotiable; that is, it can be exchanged for cash. Thus, bond certificates belong in a safe, yours or your broker's.

There are two ways you can make a profit trading bonds: on the coupon (the interest rate) and on the appreciation of the bond itself. If you purchase a five-year $1,000 bond at par ($1,000) with a 7 percent coupon, you will not only get your $1,000 back at the end of the five years, you'll receive 7 percent interest per year in the meantime. If you purchase a five-year $1,000 bond at par with a 7 percent coupon and during the holding period the value of the bond rises, you can sell it at a profit before it matures. When making this decision, you must weigh the benefits of receiving the profit now against the total interest you would earn by holding the bond to maturity.

Bonds seem pretty safe, and are considered a conservative investment, but don't forget that to make income, you must assume risk. The risk with bonds is that the maker (the government, municipality, or corporation) will default on the loan. It doesn't happen often, but it does happen. Ratings services such as Moodys and Standard & Poors, evaluate bonds for quality and safety and assign ratings like B, A, AA, AAA. Check a bond's rating before you buy.

Cash

In times of uncertainty cash is king. It is always wise to keep a portion of your portfolio in cash, but how much? Harry Browne's *Why the Best-Laid Investment Plans Usually Go Wrong* is probably the best book to start with when beginning to set up your portfolio mix. Browne gives a thorough but easy-to-understand guide to creating both a permanent and a speculative portfolio and helps you analyze how much of your assets to assign to each. Use his guidelines as a starting point, and do your own testing on the concepts.

Futures (Commodities and Financials)

"Futures trading is speculative and includes risk of loss." The Commodity Futures Trading Commission (CFTC) and the NFA require that all commodities trading advisors,

(CTAs) include this statement in any material they send out. This statement is required with good reason. The ability to trade large dollar contracts with small dollar outlay (margin) magnifies any gains or losses you might experience. Because commodities are traded on margin, people say they are very volatile. That is not quite true; if you traded each and every commodity contract for its full cash value, it would not really be volatile. The size of the move you observe depends on the power of the magnifying glass you use.

Futures trading offers a unique high-risk, high-return investment medium for seasoned traders. Don't ever lose sight of the fact that it is like buying a $100,000 house with $5,000. To further complicate the deal, futures contracts expire. That is, you are obligated to complete your transaction within a specified period of time. Thus, it is like buying that house and knowing you must sell it within the next three months.

All the basics of futures trading are presented in *Getting Started in Futures* by Todd Lofton. Lofton does a great job of explaining everything you need to know to get started, including providing an in-depth look at each futures contract.

Mutual Funds

A mutual fund is like a cooperative: a group of investors pooling their money can purchase stocks, bonds, or other investments that each alone could not afford. The mutual fund is managed by a professional investment company; you pay the company a fee for structuring and running the "collective" for you. Developed in 1924, mutual funds have grown to have specialties such as stock index funds, gold funds, bond funds, and more.

As a trader, you can time the market, time the economy, or time sectors within the economy and buy and sell mutual funds to take advantage of these moves. The advantage to you of using mutual funds is that you usually can participate with a much smaller cash outlay than if you were trading the stock, bond, or futures directly. The disadvantage is that you will have to pay fees to the management company as well as brokerage fees to buy and sell the mutual fund.

In analyzing mutual funds, you will want to gather your data, chart it historically, and follow the same process as if you were trading a stock, bond, or futures contract. You will still be looking for a system to reveal buy and sell opportunities, testing your system exhaustively, and following the system once it's developed.

Many mutual fund management companies permit switching, although some funds have disallowed the practice. Mutual fund switching means that you have established an account that stays at a particular management company, which has several funds, say sector funds, a gold fund, and a stock fund. Presumably the company also has a money market fund that allows you to put your money in cash rather than in any of the designated funds. As your analysis of each fund shows buying and selling opportunities, you can move your money out of one fund and into another, usually without incurring much more than a small transfer fee. In other words, you are switching your money back and forth between funds while keeping it at one management company.

Mutual Fund Switch Strategies & Timing Tactics by Warren Boroson is one of the Investor's Self-Teaching Seminars by Probus Publishing. This book will lead you through the step-by-step process of learning to trade mutual funds by timing and switching.

Options

Often thought to be the "safe" way to trade, options are about as safe as skydiving. Yeah, you have a parachute, but your time frame for using it is limited.

Options can be considered portfolio insurance, or they can be used as a purely speculative venture on their own.

Let's start with an example. You own 100 shares of IBM, which you bought at 50. IBM is now selling for 100. The market seems to be vulnerable and you do not want to lose your profit. Since you are not certain that the market will continue to go up, you can purchase *put options* on IBM that will act as insurance. A put option is a contract that allows an owner to sell a fixed number of underlying security of futures contracts at a fixed price and a fixed time period. If the price of IBM goes down, the value of your options goes up, theoretically covering the loss in the stock.

That seems simple enough: If you have a put option, you want the price of the underlying stock to go down; if you have a *call option*, you want the price of the underlying stock to go up. So where is the risk?

The value of an option decays with time. As the time for the option to expire approaches, its speculative value decreases. If the value of the option were the linear inverse of the price of the stock, one's straight line upward would be matched with the other's straight line downward, but that is not the case. (See Figure 9.1.)

The risk is that you have properly determined the direction of the market and nevertheless lose the *premium* because it expires before the market reaches your goal.

This is not pencil-and-paper stuff. Watching the ever-volatile options market and factoring in all the variables requires a computer and a software package that specializes in options. OptionVue and Optionomics both have software for this purpose. Institute for Options Research, Inc., and Options Institute have software, books, and training for options trading.

David L. Caplan, of Opportunities in Options, authored a 45-page pamphlet, which you can get for free just by calling him. The pamphlet, entitled "Profiting with

 put option
the right, but not the obligation, to sell shares at the exercise price on or before the expiration date.

 call option
contract that gives the buyer of the option the right, but not the obligation, to take delivery of the underlying security at a specific price within a certain time.

 premium
price a buyer pays to an option writer for granting an option contract.

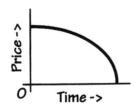

FIGURE 9.1 Time value of options.

Futures Options," gives four tables that are particularly valuable for options traders. For a quick overview of options trading, contact Caplan for the pamphlet.

There are two books you must read before trading options: *Getting Started in Options* by Michael C. Thomsett and *Options as a Strategic Investment* by Lawrence G. McMillan. The first book is an easy-reading, how-to guide to getting started in options trading. After you understand this one, study the second book. McMillan's book is thorough and complex but is the definitive work on options trading, specifically the Black-Scholes equations; they are all in McMillan.

Stocks

When you buy a share of stock, you are becoming an owner of the company that issued the stock. That is putting it simply, but all too often we forget there is a company and a product behind our trade.

Do not take hot tips from friends or brokers; stock trading is not a game. If you are a fundamental analyst, do your research on the company you are buying; if you are a technician, analyze your charts.

Stock picking can be an arduous task. There are over 20,000 stocks from which you can choose. One way to approach this monumental task is with computer software. Yahoo! Finance, Hoover's, TeleChart 2000, and Radar Screen offer methods to specify parameters to search for and let the computer do the scanning. For instance, you might want to narrow your analysis to only those stocks whose price is 3 percent higher than it was last month, or to stocks that are below their 50-day moving average. Again, any theory you develop about what makes individual stock prices move must be thoroughly tested. Do not make the mistake of thinking that stock trading is simpler or less risky than other types of trading and try to skip your homework.

There are lots and lots of books you can read about the stock market. I suggest you start with *The Intelligent Investor* by Benjamin Graham and then read *The Stock Market* by Richard Teweles.

INVESTMENT TIMING

Timing is everything. If you buy the right stuff at the right time, you make money. If you buy the right stuff at the wrong time, you lose money.

One book stands out above all the rest when it comes to the broad picture of timing: *Strategic Investment Timing* by Dick A. Stoken. This book is an in-depth but easy-to-understand analysis of long-term timing strategies. Stoken addresses economic cycles and methods of profiting from each phase. He shows you when to buy and sell stocks and bonds, when to have your assets in cash, when to trade commodities, and when to buy and sell real estate.

CONTRARY INVESTING

Contrary investing means you figure out what everyone else is doing and you do the opposite. As J. Paul Getty said in *How to Be Rich*, "Buy when everyone else is selling, and hold until everyone else is buying." This is more than just a catchy slogan. It is the very essence of successful investment.

This is all well and good if you have a way of telling what everyone else is doing. For the most part, aggressive contrary investing is tantamount to predicting tops and bottoms; it cannot be done. To be successful as a contrarian you need to be able to scale into your trades and wait out the completion of the trend. For instance, contrarians started shorting the stock market in 1986. It was the right idea, but too soon. Even though it was "overvalued," the market continued up until October of 1987. To be a successful contrarian in that example, you would have needed a tremendous amount of capital to continue adding to your short positions until the market finally crashed.

Nevertheless, contrary advice is useful if you are employing it not to predict the future but to avoid lemming behavior. Do not follow the crowd; be your own guru. Your studies and extensive testing, not the mania and panic reactions of people in groups, will tell you what to invest in.

For a practical, commonsense look at contrary investing, pick up a copy of *Contrary Investing—The Insider's Guide to Buying Low and Selling High* by Richard E. Band.

Chapter

Selecting a Computer

PC OR MACINTOSH?

Unless you have a scientific application that requires the power of a Cray computer, you should first choose your software and then purchase the computer that will optimally run that software. (Crays don't come with software; you have to write your own.)

At last count there were over 200 popular financial software products that run on PCs (IBM or compatible) and 3 financial software products that run on the Macintosh platform.

With only 1.5 percent of the software products running on Macs, it makes sense to buy a PC—if you only look at that piece of information. But if you have an idea what software you want to use, and what market application you are interested in and it's available on the Macintosh—then you should buy a Mac.

The American Association of Individual Investors publishes a book called *The Individual Investor's Guide to Computerized Investing*. In the back of the book are "Investment Software Grids" that list all of the PC software and all of the Macintosh software for traders/investors.

When purchasing a new computer, buy the most you can afford with respect to processing power and disk space. Personal computers get cheaper every year, and software grows to fill the available space. My personal preference is to devote one computer to trading and have nothing else running on it. Even though you are free to run in a multiprocessing environment, I don't put anything else on my trading computer. I wouldn't want to take a chance on one piece of software having a bug that could interfere in any way with my trading software or data. (All software has bugs. It is a logical impossibility to create bug-free code.)

If you already have a computer that you want to use for your trading, and you don't want to purchase a new one, then use the AAII guide or *Traders' Catalog & Resource Guide* as a resource and start collecting demos. If you don't have a computer, you can rent one or use a friend's or go to a place like Kinko's Copy Center where you can use their computers. The only way you will really know what software you like is to try it.

Every decision you make should involve Benjamin Franklin's decision-tree process. Make a list of your "musts" and your "wants." What features must your trading computer have? What features would you like it to have? Create a grid and start asking questions. Go to your local computer store and window shop. Keep the pros and the cons in the grid.

You will want to know details about cast and features. You will want to know what the minimum computer configuration is for each software demo you've ordered. Let's say that one piece of software needs a 386 processor and 4 MB of memory and uses 5 MB of disk space on your hard drive. A second piece of software needs a Pentium processor with 8 MB of memory and uses 30 MB of storage. Does bigger always mean better? Not necessarily. In this case, you will probably be paying more for the computer and more for the software, but it does not necessarily mean that you will make more trading profits. (And that is our only real concern, remember?)

All of the information you get from the hardware vendors must be put into a table for you to use in your final analysis. You don't want to buy a lot more computer than you need, but at the same time, you don't want to get a computer that you will outgrow soon.

MB
abbreviation for megabyte. A megabyte is 1,024 kilobytes, or roughly 1 million bytes.

MFGR	TOTAL PRICE	Pentium	14" VGA Color Monitor	1.44 MB 3.5" Floppy Drive	1 Gig. Hard Drive	16 MB RAM	CD-ROM 4x	Tape Backup

FIGURE 10.1   Fill in the prices for each option and add up the total.

Figure 10.1 presents the format I would use while inquiring about computer hardware.

To keep from getting really confused, make sure you compare oranges with oranges. If your list includes computers of widely differing configurations it will be impossible to compare price. A way to solve that problem is to ask each manufacturer in writing for a quote on a specific configuration.

Offhand I know of more than 50 hardware manufacturers you can call to get information. Or, if you prefer, most computer software stores carry a periodical called *Computer Shopper*, which is a huge catalog of hardware of all kinds.

Chapter 11

Selecting Software

The software you choose for your data analysis and system testing is your toolbox. It is not the end of your thinking and theorizing, it is the beginning. Some people think that when they finally get to the software stage that they are done, that the computer will do the thinking for them. Not so.

Computers will never (mark my word) take the place of the human brain. That is a sci-fi fantasy perpetuated by people who do not understand how computers work. A computer is limited by the human who is conceptualizing and programming it. It will not reach out on its own and imagine new scenarios.

The human brain can imagine. Furthermore, each and every human brain imagines differently. It is this diversity of imagination that makes the market. Some people think it is time to sell while others think it is time to buy. I have talked with hundreds, maybe even thousands, of traders and never once found that any one of them had the same system as any other. In fact, no two have even agreed on what moves the market.

The software I am addressing in this chapter is the kind that will be the tool for your imagination to use in simplifying calculations and charting. A computer really is just a very fast adding machine. We use it in trading to make our lives easier, so we do not have to sit and watch the ticker tape with pen and paper in hand making manual calculations. The computer can do all this much faster. Nevertheless, it will do only what you tell it to do.

It is very easy to allow the software selection process to become your main focus and to let your trading become secondary. If software analysis becomes your goal, and not the means to your goal, change your job title from trader to software reviewer.

Better and better software will not necessarily improve your trading. Buying a better camera will not make you a better photographer. You can become a better photographer by taking classes and practicing; you can become a better trader by taking classes and practicing. Good classes in photography are more readily available than good classes in trading, so for the most part you will be reading and studying on your own.

Software selection assumes that you already have determined your trading focus. If you focus on trading options, you will want different software than if you focus on trading mutual funds. If you focus on trading commodity futures, you will want different software from either of the above.

If you go to your local computer store looking for software, you will not find much. Very few of the trading products have made it to the shelves. From that perspective, you might think that no such software is available. That could not be further from the truth. There are, at my last count, 432 software products specifically directed to investing and trading. They just are not in the computer stores.

Trading software can be found in special interest magazines, catalogs, and resource guides. I keep the most up-to-date list of all trading software products in the *Traders' Catalog & Resource Guide* and on the Internet at The Money Mentor, along with descriptions and reviews. For the most part, trading software is acquired by mail order. If you go to trade shows and conferences related to trading, you usually can find many vendors with their latest products and demonstration units. Otherwise, call the vendor, ask for a demo disk if they have one, try that out for a day or two, and then order the software over the phone.

Again, every decision you make should involve Benjamin Franklin's decision-tree process. Make a list of your "musts" and your "wants." What features *must* your trading software have? What features would you *like* (or want) it to have? Create a grid and start using each of the demos you've ordered. As you use the software, write down what is good about it and what is bad about it. Keep the pros and the cons in the grid.

I like to assign a value from 0 to 10 to each item under consideration, with 0 being "worthless" and 10 being "must." That way, when you've completed the grid, you can add up all the numbers and have a simple value comparison.

For instance, here is a simple table to begin with:

Program Name: _____

Ease of Use	(0–10)	_____
Technical Indicators	(0–10)	_____
Computational Speed	(0–10)	_____
Graphics Capabilities	(0–10)	_____
Documentation	(0–10)	_____
Customer Support	(0–10)	_____

When I first began my research, I made a spreadsheet with every feature of every demo I ordered and compared them all to each other in great detail. I continue to update that table, and from time to time I publish it in the *Traders' Catalog & Resource Guide* or on the Internet. Doing the work yourself will give you a much better idea of the functionality of each demo and how comfortable you are with its workings. The table is much too extensive to publish here, but if you would like to look at my research, feel free to check either source; it is updated every six months or so. A portion of it is reproduced in Table 11.1 later in this chapter.

	AIQ Trading Expert	Investor's FastTrack	Windows on Wall Street	MarketView	SuperCharts	TradeStation	OptionVue IV	First Alert	Options to Win
TIME FRAME									
Delayed									◆
End of Day	◆	◆	◆		◆	◆	◆		◆
Historical				◆	◆			◆	
Real Time—any time frame				◆		◆	◆	◆	◆
Real Time—selected time frames									
DATA VENDORS SUPPORTED									
ASCII									
Bonneville							◆	◆	
CompuTrac									
CSI	◆				◆	◆			
Data Broadcasting Corp.	◆					◆	◆	◆	
Dial Data	◆		◆						
Dow Jones	◆		◆	◆				◆	
FutureSource									
Knight-Ridder					◆	◆		◆	
MetaStock									
PC Quote	◆							◆	
Platt's					◆			◆	
Reuters					◆			◆	
S&P Comstock					◆		◆	◆	◆
Telekurs					◆				
Telerate									
Tick Data						◆			

Table 11.1   Software Comparison Table

Table 11.1 Continued

	AIQ Trading Expert	Investor's FastTrack	Windows on Wall Street	MarketView	SuperCharts	TradeStation	OptionVue IV	First Alert	Options to Win
TRADING SYSTEM									
Black Box									
Gray Box	◆								
White Box			◆		◆	◆			
TRADING SYSTEM ANALYSIS & CREATION									
Back-testing		◆	◆		◆	◆		◆	
Optimization		◆							
Programming Language		◆			◆	◆			
User Programmable			◆		◆	◆			◆
NEWS									
Alerts							◆		◆
Dial-up (Modem)			◆	◆					
Online			◆	◆					◆
ACCOUNT MANAGEMENT									
Client Account Management	◆			◆			◆	◆	
Personal Account Management	◆						◆	◆	
Performance Summary	◆	◆			◆	◆	◆	◆	
Positions Log	◆	◆			◆	◆	◆	◆	◆
Statistical Analysis		◆			◆	◆	◆		
Variable # contracts					◆	◆	◆	◆	◆
MONEY MANAGEMENT									
Optimal-f									
Portfolio Management				◆				◆	
What-if Analysis							◆		

Table 11.1   Continued

	AIQ Trading Expert	Investor's FastTrack	Windows on Wall Street	MarketView	SuperCharts	TradeStation	OptionVue IV	First Alert	Options to Win
NEURAL NETWORK									
Back Propagation									
Excel Interface									
ALERTS									
Calendar								♦	
News & Information									
Price	♦						♦		♦
Time	♦						♦		
Volume	♦						♦		♦
SPREADSHEET INTERFACE									
ASCII Text File	♦	♦							
DDE Link							♦		♦
Excel		♦					♦		♦
Lotus		♦							♦
TOOLS									
% Retracement			♦		♦	♦			♦
Angle of Trend Line					♦	♦			♦
Andrews' Pitchfork			♦						♦
Channels	♦		♦		♦	♦			♦
Cycle Arcs					♦				♦
Cycle Lines			♦		♦	♦			♦
Ellipse					♦	♦			♦
Fibonacci Fan Lines			♦		♦	♦			♦
Fibonacci Time Zones			♦		♦	♦			♦

	AIQ Trading Expert	Investor's FastTrack	Windows on Wall Street	MarketView	SuperCharts	TradeStation	OptionVue IV	First Alert	Options to Win
Table 11.1 Continued									
TOOLS									
Gann Angles			♦		♦	♦		♦	
Horizontal Lines			♦		♦	♦		♦	
Linear Regression			♦		♦	♦		♦	
Parallel Lines					♦	♦		♦	
Rectangles					♦	♦		♦	
Speed/Resistance Lines			♦		♦	♦		♦	
Standard Deviation		♦	♦		♦	♦		♦	
Support/Resistance									
Text			♦		♦	♦		♦	
Trend Lines	♦	♦	♦		♦	♦		♦	
INDICATORS									
Accumulation Swing Index			♦	♦	♦	♦			
Accumulation-Distribution	♦		♦		♦	♦		♦	
ADX	♦		♦		♦	♦		♦	
Alpha Beta Trend									
Andrews' Pitchfork			♦					♦	
Arms Ease of Movement									
Arms Equivolume									
Average Range Channel					♦	♦		♦	
Average True Range		♦		♦	♦	♦		♦	
Baskets—user definable				♦	♦	♦		♦	
Bollinger Bands	♦		♦		♦	♦		♦	
Chaikin Oscillator			♦						

Table 11.1   Continued

	AIQ Trading Expert	Investor's FastTrack	Windows on Wall Street	MarketView	SuperCharts	TradeStation	OptionVue IV	First Alert	Options to Win
INDICATORS									
Commodity Channel Index	♦		♦	♦	♦	♦		♦	
Commodity Selection			♦		♦	♦			
Correlation Analysis									♦
Daily Range			♦	♦	♦	♦		♦	
Demand Index					♦				
Detrended Price Oscillator		♦	♦	♦		♦		♦	
Difference Line					♦	♦		♦	
Dividend Yield Matrix		♦						♦	
Division Line				♦					
DMI (Directional Movement)	♦		♦	♦	♦	♦		♦	
Equivolume	♦							♦	
Fibonacci Movement			♦		♦	♦		♦	
Fourier Transform									
Gapless Bar Chart					♦	♦			
Hal Momentum									
Herrick Payoff Index			♦		♦	♦			
Japanese Candlesticks	♦		♦		♦	♦		♦	
Key Reversal					♦	♦		♦	
MACD	♦	♦	♦		♦	♦		♦	
Market Profile				♦				♦	
Mass Index				♦					
McClellan Oscillator	♦				♦	♦			
McClellan Summation Index	♦								
Median Price			♦		♦	♦		♦	

Table 11.1 Continued

INDICATORS	AIQ Trading Expert	Investor's FastTrack	Windows on Wall Street	MarketView	SuperCharts	TradeStation	OptionVue IV	First Alert	Options to Win
MFI	♦		♦		♦	♦			
Momentum	♦	♦	♦	♦	♦	♦		♦	
Momentum Oscillator	♦	♦	♦	♦	♦	♦		♦	
Money Flow Index	♦		♦		♦	♦		♦	
Moving Average—1 line	♦		♦	♦	♦	♦		♦	
Moving Average—2 lines			♦	♦	♦	♦		♦	
Moving Average—3 lines			♦	♦	♦	♦		♦	
Moving Average—displaced			♦		♦	♦			
Moving Average—envelopes			♦		♦	♦		♦	
Moving Average—exponential		♦	♦	♦	♦	♦		♦	
Moving Average—weighted			♦		♦	♦		♦	
Negative Volume Index	♦		♦					♦	
On Balance Volume	♦		♦	♦	♦	♦		♦	
Open Interest	♦		♦	♦	♦	♦		♦	
Option Analysis	♦			♦				♦	
Overlays—different technical studies			♦		♦	♦		♦	
Overlays—different markets			♦		♦	♦		♦	
Overlays—different time frames					♦	♦		♦	
Overlays—different values of same study			♦		♦	♦		♦	
PaintBar					♦	♦			
Parabolic SAR			♦	♦	♦	♦		♦	
Percent Change	♦		♦		♦	♦		♦	
Percent R			♦	♦	♦	♦		♦	

Table 11.1 Continued

INDICATORS	AIQ Trading Expert	Investor's FastTrack	Windows on Wall Street	MarketView	SuperCharts	TradeStation	OptionVue IV	First Alert	Options to Win
Pivot Points					♦	♦			
Point & Figure			♦	♦	♦	♦		♦	
Positive Volume Index	♦		♦						
Price & Volume Trend	♦		♦					♦	
Price Channel					♦	♦		♦	
Printing	♦		♦	♦	♦	♦		♦	
Range Leaders					♦	♦			
Rate of Change			♦		♦	♦		♦	
Ratio									
Regression			♦		♦	♦		♦	
RSI	♦	♦	♦	♦	♦	♦		♦	
Speed/Resistance			♦		♦	♦		♦	
Spread			♦	♦	♦	♦		♦	
Standard Deviation	♦	♦	♦	♦	♦	♦		♦	
Stochastic—fast	♦	♦	♦	♦	♦	♦		♦	
Stochastic—slow	♦	♦	♦	♦	♦	♦		♦	
Stochastic—variable %K, %D	♦	♦	♦		♦	♦		♦	
Swing Accumulation									
Swing High/Swing Low			♦		♦	♦			
Swing Index			♦	♦	♦	♦			
Swing SAR									
Theoretical Value	♦							♦	
Tick Size (incremental volume)					♦	♦	♦	♦	
Tick Volume					♦	♦	♦	♦	

Table 11.1 Continued									
	AIQ Trading Expert	*Investor's FastTrack*	*Windows on Wall Street*	*MarketView*	*SuperCharts*	*TradeStation*	*OptionVue IV*	*First Alert*	*Options to Win*
INDICATORS									
Time & Sales (tick chart)				◆	◆	◆		◆	
Time Series Forecast									
Trade Volume Index					◆				
Trend Lines	◆	◆	◆	◆	◆	◆		◆	
TRIX			◆						
Ultimate Oscillator				◆		◆	◆	◆	
Up/Down Average				◆	◆	◆	◆	◆	
Up/Down Tick Difference				◆		◆	◆	◆	
Vol %	◆								
Volatility SAR				◆		◆	◆	◆	
Volatility, Historical	◆					◆		◆	
Volume	◆		◆	◆	◆	◆		◆	
Volume Accumulation/Dist	◆								
Volume Oscillator	◆		◆			◆	◆	◆	
Volume Rate-of-Change			◆			◆	◆		
Weighted Close			◆			◆	◆	◆	
What-if Analysis	◆	◆					◆	◆	
Williams Ultimate Oscillator									
Williams' %R	◆		◆			◆	◆		
Zigzag	◆		◆			◆	◆		
DATA MAINTENANCE									
Automated	◆	◆	◆	◆		◆	◆	◆	
Continuous Contract				◆		◆	◆	◆	

Table 11.1   Continued

	AIQ Trading Expert	Investor's FastTrack	Windows on Wall Street	MarketView	SuperCharts	TradeStation	OptionVue IV	First Alert	Options to Win
DATA MAINTENANCE									
Edit	◆		◆	◆	◆	◆		◆	
Manual	◆		◆	◆	◆	◆		◆	
Merge	◆		◆	◆	◆	◆		◆	
Translation/Format Converter	◆	◆	◆	◆	◆	◆		◆	
GRAPHICS									
Color	◆	◆	◆	◆	◆	◆	◆	◆	
Date & Time Axis	◆		◆	◆	◆	◆		◆	
Date Axis		◆	◆		◆	◆		◆	
Date Axis forward in time								◆	
Fonts, variable				◆	◆	◆		◆	
Grids, variable				◆	◆	◆		◆	
Multiple Monitors					◆	◆		◆	
Multiple Windows/Charts			◆	◆	◆	◆		◆	
Overlay Charts				◆	◆	◆		◆	
Overlays of Differing Time Frames					◆	◆		◆	
Quote Window						◆		◆	
SYSTEM LIBARY									
Borland C									
Library Functions					◆				
OPERATING SYSTEM									
Macintosh									
OS/2								◆	
Windows				◆		◆	◆		
UNIX									

Table 11.1 Continued

	AIQ Trading Expert	Investor's FastTrack	Windows on Wall Street	MarketView	SuperCharts	TradeStation	OptionVue IV	First Alert	Options to Win
UTILITIES									
DDE (Dynamic Data Exchange)			◆			◆		◆	
Filter Quotes	◆							◆	
Ranking Quotes		◆						◆	
Sorting Quotes		◆						◆	
Spreads Matrix (spreads, straddles, & ratios)									◆
Ticker Tape								◆	
OPTIONS ANALYSIS									
Automatic Strikes, Expiration Cycles							◆		
Black-Scholes	◆						◆	◆	
Delta, Gamma, Theta, Vega							◆		
Flexible Quotes Display							◆		
Futures Options							◆		
Graphic Position Analysis							◆		
Implied Volatility	◆						◆	◆	
Index Options							◆		
Optiman Position Recommendation							◆	◆	

Later in this book I discuss "canned" trading systems—that is, systems that someone else has developed and that you purchase. This chapter is not for that. Here we will take a quick look at some of the best-selling software products that can help you develop your own trading system.

FITNESS FOR PURPOSE

Financial software is available that will address nearly any aspect of the markets in which you are interested. Software that is general in nature and of mass-market interest is inexpensive; software that is designed for a narrow, specific audience is usually very expensive.

In the beginning of your trading career, it makes sense to acquire software with which you can grow and learn. Two popular products are available that will get you started for minimal dollar outlay and from which you can expand to their professional products at a later time.

MetaStock for Windows, a product of Equis International (800-882-3040 x55), runs on IBM and compatible computers. MetaStock is clean, simple, and intuitive. You can install it in just a few minutes and begin using it right away. MetaStock is Microsoft Office compatible, a high standard to meet and is object oriented. By that I mean you can click on an object such as a moving average, and drag it to another chart. You do not have to go through a maze of computerese setup steps. MetaStock provides more technical analysis indicators than you could ever need as well as a simple development language for creating your own indicators and testing your system ideas.

Equis International offers a variety of companion products for traders, including The Downloader, The Technician, Pulse, MetaStock Real-Time, and a host of educational products. When your trading moves from the learning stage to the professional stage, you can graduate into MetaStock Real-Time without losing all the work you've done in MetaStock.

SuperCharts, from Omega Research (305) 485-7000, is also a Windows product, running on IBMs and clones. The big brother of SuperCharts is called TradeStation, and is Omega's real-time analysis product. Both of these products are easy to install and intuitive to use, and both use Omega's Easy Language for developing your own systems and indicators.

Both MetaStock and SuperCharts run between $300 and $400. Frankly, as a software designer, I don't know how either of them can sell such powerful analysis software so inexpensively. Each has a tremendous amount of person-time and research behind them.

Newer to the technical analysis software shelves are two products, one for Macintosh and one for Windows. Investor/RT, by Linn Software, is for Macs and is impressive in its scope. It provides real-time, delayed, or end-of-day analysis, portfolio management, and screening in addition to the vast array of technical analysis tools and magnificent charting capabilities. TickerWatcher ranges in price from $395 to $695, depending on the optional extras you choose.

Heir to the CompuTrac tradition, SMARTrader is an all-purpose, easy-to-use technical analysis software program for Windows, developed by former employees of CompuTrac. Intuitive and simple in design, SMARTrader has all the bells and whistles and at its introductory price of $199 is very inexpensive.

Worden Brothers, Inc. makes their technical analysis software, TeleChart 2000, available for next to nothing. It usually is available for $29, although I have seen it as low as $19.95. So how do they stay in business? You get your data from them—and even that is incredibly cheap. Their data runs anywhere from $2.50 per month to $19 per month. While TeleChart 2000 is not available in a real-time version, their end-of-day technical analysis is quite respectable.

The four other software products mentioned in this chapter require an outside vendor for data transmission, whether it is end-of-day or real time. See the next chapter for a list of data sources and compatible software.

THROWAWAYS

All of the software just mentioned is so inexpensive in the overall scheme of things that you can begin with any one of them and throw it away when you are ready to graduate. This is not to say that you will need to do so, as each of them is sufficient for advanced analysis. But if you spend the early part of your education with these products and find that you want to specialize in a more narrow facet of trading, you certainly have not wasted your money. Everything you learn with these products is applicable throughout your trading career.

I could write volumes on the myriad of software products available to traders, but others have beat me to it and you should benefit from their expert analysis. These books in particular are devoted to the exposition of trading software:

✔ *The Individual Investor's Guide to Computerized Investing* is updated annually by the American Association of Individual Investors, a nonprofit educational organization. In this guide you can find a complete list of products and descriptions, along with prices and phone numbers.

✔ *Computer Analysis of the Futures Market* by Chuck LeBeau and David Lucas addresses practical ways to use the most common technical studies. The authors examine which studies to combine for greater profits, which signals to trade, and which need to be confirmed. The book also delves into uses of popular analysis software such as Meta-Stock, Telescan, SuperCharts, and more.

✔ *The Stock Market Investor's Computer Guide* by Michael Gianturco explains in clear, simple English the pros and cons of a wide range of computer hardware and software as well as offering a clear explanation of what computers can and cannot do.

✔ *The Dow Jones-Irwin Guide to Trading Systems* by Bruce Babcock offers both an analysis of trading software and a comprehensive look at developing your own system. You should put this book on your "must" reading list, just after you have finished all the books in the beginner's section and just before you begin your software selection process.

Table 11.1 is a portion of one I update and publish in *Traders' Catalog & Resource Guide* every six months or so. As with my other research, I also make this table available at my Internet site, in its most up-to-date configuration. This table began years ago as my first decision-tree analysis of trading software. It has expanded greatly since then, including the widest range of software and capabilities you can imagine. Studying this table will save you months and months of work. Note that I am including only a few of the best of the vast number of vendors, due to the space limitations of this book. If you want to see the full list, go to The Money Mentor on the Internet, where paper is not a limitation.

STILL CONFUSED?

If you still have questions about what computer or software to buy, give us a call at (760) 930-1050 or toll-free 888-68-SUNNY.) We can probably point you in the right direction.

Chapter 12

Selecting a Data Source

ssuming that you have a proven system with a
positive mathematical expectation, your data are
the next most important concern. If you had the
best system in the world and fed it bad data, you would
lose money. Garbage in, garbage out, as programmers say.

The reputations and continued success are based on
the reliability and accuracy of that data. Software companies that give data away as an incentive for you to purchase their software do not necessarily have the same goal
as data vendors. Don't assume that data you get for free
are totally accurate.

WHAT ARE ACCURATE DATA?

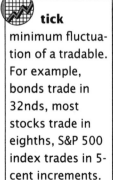

tick
minimum fluctua-
tion of a tradable.
For example,
bonds trade in
32nds, most
stocks trade in
eighths, S&P 500
index trades in 5-
cent increments.

Each and every trade executed on the floor of the exchange has a transaction time, date, quantity, and price.
Tick data, or time-and-sales data, will have all of this information.

Your broker can provide time-and-sales data (see
Figure 12.1) for a short period of time, such as a few
minutes. If the data you purchase are accurate, you will
be able to compare those data with time-and-sales
data you can get from your broker and not find any
differences.

```
010100 09:11  345.00  345.05  345.00  345.05  345.10
010100 09:12  345.10  345.15  345.10
010100 09:13  345.15  345.20  345.15  345.20
010100 09:14  345.15  345.10
```

FIGURE 12.1   Time and sales (tick) data.

Tick data are used to create time samplings of data. For instance, the open, high, low and close of a day's trading are taken from the first tick, the highest tick, the lowest tick, and the final tick of the day. A 15-minute bar is constructed from the first tick and the last tick of that time period. (See Figure 12.2.) If your tick data are not accurate, the longer-term data will not be either.

If you are going to be using daily data (see Figure 12.3), especially in the beginning of your learning curve, compare your data with data printed in the *Wall Street Journal, Investor's Business Daily,* or *Barrons.* We collect data each day from one of these papers (they do not print historical data), but it will be well worth your time.

Date	Time	Open	High	Low	Close
010100	09:00	345.15	345.30	345.10	345.25
010100	09:15	345.25	345.50	345.10	345.35
010100	09:30	345.35	345.40	345.25	345.35

FIGURE 12.2   15-minute data.

Date	Open	High	Low	Close
010100	345.15	345.30	345.10	345.25
010200	345.25	345.50	345.10	345.35
010300	345.35	345.40	345.25	345.35

FIGURE 12.3   Daily data.

Compare several sources of data before you lock into a single source forever. The extra step of verifying your data is as important as verifying your system.

Chapter 3 covers the sources of information and data. There is no need to repeat that material here. Contact each data vendor for literature and pricing, or go to The Money Mentor on the Internet (www.moneymentor.com): A virtual home page for each vendor is available, with information supplied by the vendors.

Chapter 13

Purchasing a Canned Trading System

A canned trading system is one that someone else has designed, presumably tested, implemented either via computer software or an explicit manual, and now offers for sale. Most often the price of the system is in direct proportion to its efficacy. If a system is likely to make you a great deal of money, the vendor will charge a lot for it.

I break the universe of canned systems into three categories—black boxes, gray boxes, and white boxes—depending on how much of the inner workings of the system are revealed to the buyer. A black box does not reveal any of the inner mechanics of the system; you buy it, you trade it blindly, that's all. The vendor of a gray box will tell you some of the theory behind what the system does but not reveal all of its inner workings. By contrast, a white box is a fully revealed system. The vendor of a white-box system will tell you everything there is to know about the way this system is designed and implemented.

The first two, black and gray boxes, will be sold to you as a fax service, as a hotline, or as software. The authors cannot tell you how to trade either of these methods without revealing all the secrets. A white box can take many forms, including fax services, hotlines, software, and documentation.

CONFIDENTIALITY

When you purchase a system, the contract that comes with it usually includes a secrecy clause; it is important to honor that contract. Any time you purchase something intended for a single user and share it with your friends, you are stealing. Furthermore, you are putting the vendor out of business. Developers can continue to supply the market with products only if they have the funds to promote research, development, and marketing.

Second, if you contribute to the proliferation of a system by offering it to friends, you are participating in the system's demise and cutting your own throat. If enough people begin trading the same system, the system will not continue working. If everyone came to the market to buy and no one wanted to sell, because they were all looking at the same signals, that would be the end of that system.

In fact, as a student of the markets, you can see that market theories come and go in waves as they catch on and then fade from popularity. The wider acceptance the theory gains, the less it works. It is sort of like all the passengers running to one side of the boat; eventually it will tip over.

EVALUATING CANNED SYSTEMS

If the vendor will not tell you how the system works, how do you know it is any good? There are several ways to answer this question. Ask the vendor for a track record of the system's historical performance. Ask whether the vendor trades that same identical system himself or herself. Ask if you can test the system historically yourself. Contact the following two watchdogs.

WATCHDOGS

Two organizations, Futures Truth and Club 3000, make it their business to know how canned systems are doing. Club 3000 was so named because at the time it seemed that most systems were selling for around $3,000. Bo Thunman, the person you will want to contact at Club 3000, publishes a newsletter that compiles questions and commentary sent to him by users of various systems. Thunman is the conduit through which the world hears candid and heartfelt recommendations and complaints. John Hill, the founder of Futures Truth, tests hundreds of commercially available systems and then follows them in real-time trading. The Futures Truth analysis is available for a small fee, listing vendors and their performance records. In their comprehensive analysis process, Futures Truth developed its own extraordinarily powerful testing software, Excalibur, which is available for purchase as well.

IF THE SYSTEM'S SO GOOD WHY ARE YOU SELLING IT?

This is always the most confounding question about canned systems. Of course, the dilemma is that you will get nearly the same altruistic answer from all vendors: They are doing it out of the goodness of their hearts to help you make money. The truth is they are selling it to make money, just as you are buying it to make money. Some of the systems will make money if you follow them consistently; some will lose money no matter what you do. If you do your homework, you will know which is which.

Not all composers can sing their own music. Not all systems innovators can trade. There are brilliant, prolific inventors of systems who do not have the discipline to sit in a chair day after day and execute trades; it is more fun to be outside playing golf.

Furthermore, once you get really good at trading, it is boring. The exciting part of trading is in the learning stages and in the adrenaline phase when you are doing it wrong. Once your trading is systematic and mechanical, it makes for a pretty dull day. At that point, you can let someone else trade the system and begin the trek again by testing new theories.

BREAKING THE CODE

As a beginning trader, there is some value to purchasing a system merely to use as an example. By watching what someone else has done, not only can you begin to decipher their techniques, but you will begin to form ideas of your own with which you can experiment.

Don't waste your time trying to hack through the passwords or system protections; doing so is not worth your time and you risk prosecution.

FOLLOWING THE SYSTEM

Following someone else's system is in many ways harder than following your own. When you develop your own system, you understand how you set up the rules and often you can anticipate trades, because you know how it works. Even so, when you get in the inevitable period of *drawdown*, you will experience doubt and fear. The discipline and confidence you gained through diligent testing and research will keep you going. But when you are blind to the methodology you have purchased, it is harder to keep the faith. You have no way to know just how bad it is going to get.

drawdown
reduction in account equity as a result of a trade or series of trades.

Nevertheless, if you skip a trade (or several) or if you try to second-guess the system, you have cheated. If you do not follow each and every trade, you are not trading the system you purchased. If you lose money under these conditions, it is not the system's fault, it is yours. Worse yet, if you make more money than the system did, you will be encouraged to continue cheating. More than likely your guessing eventually will hit you with a losing streak that the system does not experience.

14

The Never-Ending Search for the Holy Grail

From time immemorial we have been looking for "the answer." Humanity has continued to search for the Holy Grail generation after generation. Only the wise know that there is no answer.

In all likelihood you will not win the lottery, you will not make a killing in the stock market, and Santa Claus will not bring you a cashier's check for a million dollars. Nevertheless, it seems to be human nature to keep hoping.

Novice and seasoned traders alike continue to search for just the right system or just the right advisor. I have observed many a new trader skip from technique to technique and from guru to guru as each one in turn fails to be the Holy Grail.

Forget it. You have all the answers you need within. Amaze yourself!

What you may not have is the discipline to organize your thoughts, test your ideas, and then follow them without wavering. But don't give up too soon; to some extent you can be trained in these aspects of trading.

In *Zen in the Markets* Edward Allen Toppel says:

> Most of us come to the market with the notion that if certain events happen, the market should react in this or that way. The market

will go up or down because of this event. Let us call this Aristotelian logic and let us promptly recognize that Aristotle belongs in universities and not in markets.

Our brains are programmed with the wrong information. We need to de-program what we learned in school about balance sheets and price earnings ratios. They do not guarantee price direction.

We must realize that the market defies logic. It has a logic all of its own, and it won't tell us in advance what its reaction to events will be. We can watch for clues and then react. Basically, the best we can hope for is quick reaction time to the market's signals. We must first wait and then follow.

Approach trading like any other new career path. You would not think you could become a successful surgeon without training. Neither can you become a successful (i.e., profitable) trader without trading. Becoming a surgeon takes 10 or more years of training! How is it that new students of the markets often hope they can become traders within months?

While no one has "the answer" but you, don't forget that you can find it only with years of research and study and experimentation.

Consider every fork of every road you take to be a learning experience, not an end to your travels.

The rules of successful trading are: Think, test, and follow. These are the phases your journey must take. Think about what you see the market doing; test your theories and design your system; then follow it religiously.

PHASE ONE: THINK

Subscribe to papers and journals and newsletters. Listen to hotlines and advisors. Read all the magazines and books you can get your hands on. BUT DON'T TRADE YET.

The market will still be there when you complete

your education. There is always another trade. But if you trade too soon, you run the risk of losing all your speculating capital and not being able to trade after your education is complete.

While you are a Phase One trader, you are like an infant learning to talk. You spend the first two years of your life listening. Likewise, spend the first phase of trading absorbing ideas. Listen to professional traders, attend seminars and workshops, but do not believe everything you hear. Absorb the information you are gathering and hold on to it; you will be evaluating it in Phase Two.

During Phase One you should watch the market but not enter any trades. Keep your charts, maintain your logs, even make *hypothetical trades* if you wish. Keep your mind open to any and all possibilities, not forming any conclusions yet about the nature of the market or the way you will trade it.

hypothetical trade
any trade not actually executed for an account.

While you are in the investigation mode, begin to collect data and observe several markets. Market vehicles all have their own character. The rhythm of the market(s) you choose to trade must match your own for you to be successful trading it. Some people like to waltz, some prefer to fox-trot, and still others enjoy the quickstep. This is a personal decision that only you can make and will require that you learn about each style before making your final choice.

For instance, if you trade individual stocks, you will hold trades longer than if you trade stock index futures. Remember, this job is about making money, and typically an individual stock will move fewer points during the day than will the stock index futures contract. A stock trader might make several trades per year; a futures trader might make several trades per day. Only you can gauge your level of comfort with the pace of the trading vehicle. For instance, the S&P 500 futures contract often moves fast and with wide swings. Consider trading this vehicle if you have nerves of steel and no heart problems. (See Figure 14.1.) For a slower-moving vehicle, note that bonds are related to interest rates and trend over long time periods. (See Figure 14.2.)

When considering a trading vehicle, I always ask the question: What's the potential hourly wage? If in the 6.5

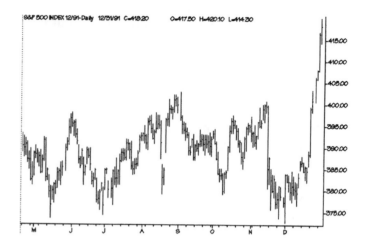

FIGURE 14.1 The S&P 500 futures contract often moves fast.

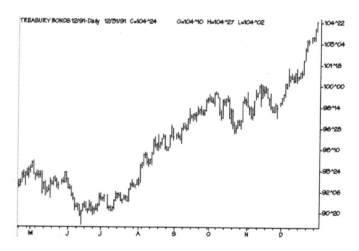

FIGURE 14.2 Bonds are related to interest rates and trend over long time periods.

hours of a trading day you can expect to make $65 profit on average, then your wage is $10 per hour. If, on the other hand, you trade a slow-moving instrument that will make you $65 per week, then in your 32.5-hour week you will make $2 per hour.

When measuring your potential dollar-per-hour wage, you need to measure how far that market moves per hour and the likelihood of your catching that move. Before measuring the speed of markets, I put all charts on the same scale. You will get a better idea of movement and rhythm if all charts are measured with the same ruler.

For instance, Figures 14.3 and 14.4 present two

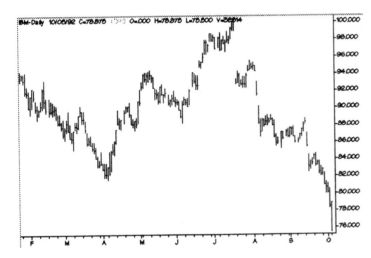

FIGURE 14.3 Chart of IBM automatically scaled by the computer.

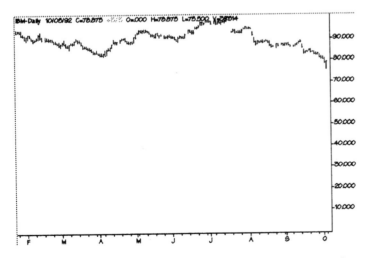

FIGURE 14.4 Chart of IBM manually scaled for potential-hourly-wage computation.

charts of IBM. The first chart is automatically scaled by the software.

I have scaled the second one manually so that the scale is 0 to 100. Visually you get a much different impression from these two charts.

I put all my charts on the same scale to make the potential hourly wage more evident.

PHASE TWO: TEST

It is time to begin generating hypotheses and conducting experiments to either verify or disprove your hypotheses. The next chapter goes into testing methods, but let's take a moment here for a brief overview.

Many technicians begin this stage with a preconceived notion and try to fit it to the market; I like to *start with the market* and try to find a notion that fits it. In Phase Two you are a researcher. Keep your lab notes as systemically as if you were a cancer researcher, remembering your high school biology techniques. Purchase one of those bound, black-and-white-marble-covered books in which to keep notes. That way you cannot cheat by tearing out pages and throwing them away.

Earlier I mentioned the potential hourly wage. This is such an important concept that you should review it before continuing.

We'll go into more depth about Phase Two in the next chapter.

PHASE THREE: FOLLOW YOUR SYSTEM

Everything you do in developing your system presupposes that you will follow it. If you are not going to follow it, why spend the time researching it? Or why spend the money buying it?

Every successful trader will agree: If you are not disciplined enough to follow the rules you have set up, you will never be successful as a trader.

Disciplined trading is like flying an airplane on instruments. You train and train on your instruments so that when you get in a precarious situation, you will have an appropriate, automatic response. (Gas is right, brake is left.) When you get in the middle of the clouds and can not see anything, you certainly do not want to override your instruments! Your fear reaction could lead you straight into a mountain. In trading, your drawdown periods are the clouds. You do not know when you will come out on the other side, and it is frightening. In spite of the fear, *follow your system.*

If you are having trouble following your system, it could be one or more of several reasons. The first reason for not following a system is that you are not sure it works. If you have not tested the system thoroughly through back-testing and forward-testing techniques, you will not trust it. And you should not!

Secondary reasons for lacking discipline are often psychologically related and can be addressed by a trader's coach or trader's psychologist. Chapter 17 addresses some of these issues.

15

Developing Your Own Trading System

It is important to be the creator of your own trading methodology because it will be designed after your personality, your willingness to accept loss, and in your own time frame.

You may like to trade every day, or you might be a long-term trader, preferring to trade on a weekly or monthly basis. You might be the kind of individual who is willing to accept a large amount of risk in order to generate large gains, or you might be willing to risk only small amounts and accept small returns as a consequence. For these reasons, you should design your own trading methods.

The most difficult part of trading is discipline. If you have designed your own system and thoroughly tested it, you will have far more luck following it than if you are attempting to follow someone else's methodology.

SYSTEM DESIGN

Developing a trading system is 10 percent inspiration and 90 percent perspiration. It is like any scientific experiment: You come up with a theory and then run experiments to try to prove or disprove the theory.

gap
time period in
which the range
is completely
above or below
the previous time
period's range.

In the very early days of my trading, I noticed that if the market was going up during the last hour of trading and in the last five minutes it moved away from that trend and went downward, the open of the next day will gap up. (A *gap* is when the market opens significantly higher or lower so that no trades were made between the open and the previous closing price.) I asked prominent traders and educators how many data points it took to prove a theory, and they all seemed to believe that 30 was sufficient.

With pen and paper (and a calculator) I tested this idea over the previous 30 days. It did great: 85 percent of the time the market responded as I had noticed! This was surely a moneymaking prospect. So, the very next day I put my money in the market, using this newfound system, and lost. I tried it again the next day, and the day after. And lost.

What was wrong? I thought I had tested enough for this to be a proven system. Back to the drawing board. I worked backward for another 30 days and found the system had only 30 percent success during that time period. Then I decided to investigate the possibility of testing concepts by computer and purchased System Writer (by Omega Research). I quickly found that this new theory of mine was valid only in the time frame in which I had observed it. Time to discard that idea and move on. In no time flat I had designed and tested dozens of systems, finding a few that worked and a lot that did not. The value of software is that you can test many more theories much faster than with a calculator. The drawback is that people tend to mistake force for power. You cannot force the computer to blast out a theory for you. You must use the power of your imagination and creativity to observe and theorize.

System design is a matter of noticing patterns, whether the patterns are chart patterns or numerical patterns or patterns involving days of the week. Pattern recognition was involved when A. Nonymous came up with the sayings:

Buy the rumor, sell the news.
Buy the new moon, sell the full moon.

Or was it sell the new moon?

System design means looking at the following set of numbers and seeing a predictable pattern:

1 2 4 8 16 32 64

Clearly the next number in sequence should be 128. How about this sequence:

1 1 2 3 5 8

This is the well-known Fibonacci sequence, which is generated by adding two adjacent numbers to form the next number. Therefore, the next number in this sequence would be 5+8, which is 13.

How about this more complex pattern:

1 11 21 1211 111221

If you can notice patterns to number sequences, you also can see them in charts, whether they are bar charts, line charts, candlestick or volume charts.

Once you spot what you think is a pattern, then you must prove or disprove your theory.

TESTING YOUR SYSTEM

Without thorough testing, you will find yourself skeptical and doubtful. You will wonder whether your system has quit working. You will find that you are fearful of accumulating losses, because you have no way of knowing when the drawdown period should end.

Do not trade any system that has not been thoroughly tested and confirmed. If you do, you are not trading to make money, you are trading for the thrill.

As a mathematician and programmer, my view of the world is based in symbolic logic and IF . . . THEN statements. I am a strong believer in cause and effect. Thus, as a trader, I view the markets in a systematic fashion, with mathematical definition. Decision trees (IF this happens,

THEN will follow, but IF the other happens, THEN something else will follow) rooted in mathematics are the basis for my trading.

Some may say that they trade on intuition, and that is their skill. My premise is that intuition is based on an unconscious set of rules and that those rules can be translated to a computer program. Those who already trade with a set of clearly defined rules can immediately translate them to a computer program.

IF it is skill that generates the profits, THEN, consciously or unconsciously, the trader has a set of rules in mind. IF the trade is following rules, THEN the system can be tested and verified.

I have met many traders who test their rules by hand, that is, with paper and pencil and sometimes a calculator. There is nothing wrong with this method except that it is very time consuming, and the tendency to give up after testing only a small subset of the data is great. Further, I find the hand-testing method prone to two types of error: wishful thinking and calculation error. Calculation error is obvious: A person makes a simple arithmetic mistake. Wishful thinking goes like this: "Oh, I would have taken that trade, even though this system doesn't show it." It is akin to outsmarting the system but is more subtle.

Another frequently used method of testing a system is through the use of a spreadsheet, such as Lotus 1-2-3 or Excel. In the beginning of my trading experience, that is exactly what I did. And, in fact, I still use spreadsheets to verify the accuracy of test results from other computer programs. The limitation with the spreadsheet method of testing is the amount of data a spreadsheet will handle and the convenience and clarity of the output.

I am adamant about testing systems. Computer testing of systems is much like running a scientific experiment. Hypotheses are generated, assumptions are made, and the experiment is set up so as not to prejudice the results with the bias of the tester.

Consider a trading system valid *only* after rigorous computer testing and verification. It must be tested over the largest set of data available. There is much discussion in the trading community about statistics: How many trades does it take to be statistically valid? As I mentioned earlier, the answer I have heard most often is 30! I could not disagree more.

My master's thesis was devoted to the subject of *curve-fitting*. Having spent years in pursuit of just the right equation to approximate the data, I also know how to avoid curve-fitting. In the futures market, to fit the historical data accurately with a polynomial equation is to restrict the degrees of freedom to the extent that future action will not be predicted correctly. In other words, the less complicated the model, the more it seems to work over time.

To test a system over a set of data that produces only 30 trades would generate a very nice model. While it would work well in the past, as the markets fluctuate and the mood changes from *bull* to bear, to sideways and back again, the model with 30 trades probably would prove accurate only over the subset of data you used for testing.

IF a system passes historical testing criteria and produces favorable results, THEN it must be traded without variation. IF the trader's testing is adequate, THEN the key to success is to hang in there. Do not give up during periods of drawdown. (See Figure 15.1.)

Drawdown is an inevitable part of trading. Com-

curve-fitting development of a set of complex mathematical or procedural rules that most closely approximate the known data or conditions.

bull market stock market that is characterized by rising prices over a long period of time. The time span is not precise, but it represents a period of investor optimism, lower interest rates, and economic growth. The opposite of a bear market.

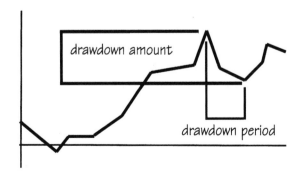

FIGURE 15.1 Equity chart showing period of drawdown.

puter testing allows the most complete and accurate analysis of market data; use it!

Computer trading is very similar to flying by instruments in an airplane. First you test your instruments, and then you test them again. Then you must rely on those instruments and follow your flight plan without regard to the fog around you. The same is true with computerized trading. Establish your system, test it, test it again, and then trust your instruments. Trading then becomes as easy as 1, 2, 3.

FACTORING IN COSTS

It is easy to pretend that we are trading in an ideal, computer-model-perfect environment while we are testing a new system. Doing so makes all the numbers look better. Without any costs, our profit is higher and our drawdown is lower. But this is not the way things behave in the real world where we are going to be trading.

To test your system under realistic conditions, you must include at least the two major costs to any trade: *commission* and *slippage*.

commission
amount of money paid to a broker for a transaction.

Commissions vary from broker to broker, full service and online. Commissions with futures brokers are negotiable. With full-service brokers, they are determined largely by how good a customer you are perceived as being. If you trade a large account frequently, you can negotiate a lower commission than if you trade a small account infrequently. A full list of all the major brokerage firms can be found in both the *Traders' Catalog* and *Resource Guide* and on the Internet at The Money Mentor. Don't hesitate to call brokers to ask for an information package and rate structure. Shop around. Again, make a grid for your decision tree. Call as many brokerage houses as you can and make your decision only when you are fully informed. (See Chapter 16.) You also can use an online broker. These brokers generally operate on a discounted commission structure, but beware! You may end up paying for a cheap trade with poor execution. It is better to

slippage
difference between the anticipated cost and the actual cost of a transaction.

pay a little more commission for a brokerage that immediately executes your trade.

Slippage is variable, and you will determine this number only after you have made a large number of trades with the broker you have chosen. Slippage happens with every middleman step. Different exchanges have different procedures, but on a typical U. S. futures exchange, you see the trade on your computer; it takes a few seconds for you to call the broker on the telephone, the broker calls the trading desk, they call the trading floor, the floor broker signals the pit, and then the trade is filled. Every step takes time. During that time, trades are being transacted rapidly on the trading floor, changing the price of the instrument you wanted to buy or sell. In electronic order routing through online brokerages, your order will be executed as soon as possible after it is received, but slippage can happen rapidly as the market continues to move even as you are placing your trade.

So that you will have a fair idea of how much slippage to factor in to your trading models and subsequent system testing, keep another spreadsheet (or add two columns to the one you already use). This time, keep track of the price at which your system told you to trade and the price at which your order actually was filled. After you have placed 20 or so trades with the broker in question, you can use the average slippage of these trades with fair confidence to represent slippage in your testing.

As I mentioned, slippage is not the same for all trading vehicles, so I cannot give you a rule of thumb here. Stock trades are first entered with your broker, and depending on the stock and its liquidity, your *fill* could vary dramatically from the price you wanted. In options trading, the broker can tell you the bid and the ask, so you can have some idea of the range your fill is likely to fall in. With futures trading, in liquid markets, the market moves quickly and you might enter an order to buy at 400 and get filled at 401. Anything is possible, and it depends not only on your broker but on how fast the market is moving when you enter your trade. In my futures trading, I'm not happy with any slippage over 1 percent.

 fill
an executed order; sometimes the term refers to the price at which an order is executed.

OPTIMIZATION

According to Ralph Vince, in *Portfolio Management Formulas*:

> Every system has certain constants. These constants can always be turned into variables and then optimized. The danger is that most systems created on past data get over-optimized, curve-fitted, to that past data, so that in hindsight the results look terrific. Yet in the real world tomorrow's optimal parameters are almost always not the same as yesterday's optimal parameters. The system that worked so well on past data falls apart in the real world.
>
> Optimization is not the enemy—abuse of optimization is.

optimization
finding the best or most favorable conditions or parameters.

Once you have determined that your system or methodology works—that is, it generates a profit over time—you can further refine it through *optimization* techniques.

For instance, if you find that a moving average crossover system is profitable with parameters of 12 and 24, your next question should be: What if the parameters were 13 and 24?

Refining the parameters of your system through optimization can be enormously time consuming. To be thorough, you should test every meaningful combination of numbers, or specifically each of the following pairs:

(2, 1),　(3, 1),　(4, 1),　(5, 1) . . . (24, 1)
(1, 2),　(3, 2),　(4, 2),　(5, 2) . . . (24, 2)

all the way to

(1, 24),　(2, 24), (3, 24),　. . .　　(23, 24)

That's a lot of testing. In fact, it would mean you need to run 529 tests (23×23). [Not 24×24 since each of the identities (1, 1), (2, 2), and so on don't cross over.]

Here is where many traders balk and decide just to "guess" that the system works and go on. Thorough testing is tedious and a very lengthy process. Once you have completed the entire testing process, however, you can trust your system.

Optimization has suffered much bad press as a result of recent advances in computer software for traders. Several software packages offer optimization routines that simplify the testing process and allow you to run 529 tests at the click of the mouse. However, these same programs, in the hands of the wrong users, can be used to fit tight curves through trading results so that the system is overfitted and will work only for a short and specific time frame.

To avoid overoptimizing, I always test my theories over three sets of data. When developing an idea, I work with the middle third of the available data. For instance, I keep tick data from the inception of the S&P 500 index futures contract, which began in April 1982. With 12 years of data I would use the period 1986 to 1989 for development. After finding a theory that works in that time frame, I would back-test using the data from the period 1982 to 1985 and forward-test using the period 1990 to 1993. In the back- and forward-tests I do not change any of the parameters discovered in developing the theory. Doing so would be curve-fitting.

If you use the entire set of data for your analysis and construct rules that map onto these data to produce optimal profits, you will be curve-fitting. Chances are this system will not work in the future.

If the system tested by the method of thirds proves profitable, then I would consider it a valid candidate for statistical analysis and money management techniques.

MONEY MANAGEMENT TECHNIQUES

Any system or trading methodology that works can be improved through proper money management techniques. As with everything else in this business, that is easy to say, but what does "works" mean?

"Works" means simply that over a long period of time, the system can be expected to make a profit. In gambling casinos, the house has a small edge; over time the house will make a profit. But it's a small edge, about 1 to 2 percent. That's all we really need in trading: a small edge. If we can be assured by mathematical and statistical means that our system has an edge, then we can use money management and discipline to provide consistently profitable results.

My favorite books on the subject of money management are written by the creative genius Ralph Vince. (Vince was once a programmer for Larry Williams.) A descendant of Leonardo da Vinci (Ralph's immigrant grandfather Americanized the last name), Vince carefully explains the theories underlying the topics and states definitively: "of the two, systems and money management, the money management is far and away more important in terms of your performance as a trader or fund manager." He also notes, however, that "Money management is predicated upon having a winning system."

Basically, Vince is saying that if you have a system that works (has a positive mathematical expectation), you can dramatically improve its profit potential by appropriately varying the number of contracts or shares you trade. There is a critical point on the curve generated by testing for the optimal number of contracts to trade; if you exceed that number, you will surely face financial ruin (and quickly at that). But if you stay on the left side of the curve, you can maximize your system's return. Vince calls the fixed fraction divisor that maximizes return "optimal-f."

While it is true that the use of optimal-f maximizes your return, it is also true that it maximizes your risk. Vince states "the greater the return (up to but not beyond the optimal-f) the greater the risk."

I have found in my own research and use of optimal-f that it is important not to use this number as a fixed constant. To utilize the theory properly, you must recompute optimal-f following the completion of each trade. Nevertheless, use of optimal-f requires the utmost discipline, as it increases drawdown in proportion to the return. (If you can not stand the heat, don't play with this fire.)

In his book *Money Management Strategies for Futures Traders*, Nauzer J. Balsara defines the percentage of capital to risk in trading thus:

$$\frac{[(A + 1)\, p] - 1}{A}$$

where A is the average payoff ratio and p is the average probability of success.

With this equation and the statistical results of your system testing, you can properly allocate your funds based on the profitability of your system.

For example, let's say you have done your homework and developed a system that is profitable 55 percent of the time. The average winning trade is $300, while the average losing trade is $100.

Your expected reward can be calculated as follows:

Expected Reward =
[% Winners × Avg $ Win] − [% Losers × Avg $ Loss]
or [55% × $300] − [45% × $100]
    = $165 − $45
    = $120.

Now solving for A,

$$[(A + 1)\, p - 1] \quad = 120$$
$$[A + 1)(.55) - 1] \quad = 120$$
$$.55\,A + .55 - 1 \quad = 120$$
$$.55A - .45 \quad = 120$$
$$.55A \quad = 119.5$$

Therefore, $A = 217.27$.

Using this information in the equation for the optimal-f fraction:

$$f = [\,(217.27 + 1)\,.55 - 1]/217.27$$
$$= 119.05\,/\,217.27$$
$$= 55\%$$

Hence, you could risk 55 percent of your current bankroll on this trade.

Balsara further discusses allocating capital across multiple commodities, a process that also lends itself to allocating capital across multiple systems. Use of either method is a form of diversification.

Both of these books are essential reading *before* you begin to trade. As stated earlier, money management is the key to the game. Any system with a positive mathematical expectation can be improved through money management techniques.

Setting Up Your Trading as a Business

DEVELOPING YOUR BUSINESS PLAN

Do not forget that you are running a business. Trading is not a hobby or a game. Starting with a book like *How to Prepare and Present a Business Plan* by Joseph R. Mancuso as a guide, develop a plan for your trading business as if you were going to present it to a finance committee. You must address not only your hopes for enormous and instant profits but the expenses you will incur immediately. It takes many years of planning and doing to become an overnight success.

In your business plan, you must consider at least the following costs:

✔ Brokerage fees
✔ Computers
✔ Data
✔ Margin requirements
✔ Office supplies
✔ Software
✔ Telephone

After determining your fixed expenses, you can dream for a moment about how much profit you'll make. Then settle down to reality and factor in the results of your system-testing predictions for profits. Do not exaggerate this number; if you do, you will only set yourself up for disappointment and failure.

Construct a spreadsheet for your break-even analysis, or use accounting paper, or even put it on plain paper. No matter what the form, get it in writing!

Break-even analysis means you determine how much money you must make to cover all your expenses. The point at which you break even is where your income exactly covers your expenses: You make no money and you lose no money.

It takes a pretty good trader to make enough money to cover overhead expenses month after month. This is not a get-rich-quick business, even though most beginning traders want it to be. (See Figures 16.1 and 16.2.)

In addition to estimates of your setup costs and monthly expenses, your business plan should include components that address structure, organization, and motivation:

✔ Overall mission statement

✔ Business objective

✔ Goals

✔ Tasks you must complete to reach your goals

End-of-Day Trader		
	Computer	$3,000
	Software	$500
	Data Feed	$50
	Telephone	$200

FIGURE 16.1 Beginning expenses for an end-of-day trader.

Real-TimeTrader		
	Computer	$3,000
	Software	$2,000
	Data Feed	$200
	Telephone	$300

FIGURE 16.2 Beginning expenses for a real-time trader.

✔ Complete and definitive rules of your trading system

✔ Statistics and mathematical results of back- and forward-testing of your trading system

✔ Money management rules

✔ Contingency plans: everything that could go wrong and everything that could go right

SELECTING A BROKER

There are many factors you will need to consider when choosing a brokerage firm to clear your trades. As with all the other business decisions you make, create a decision-tree diagram and begin your research. Call each brokerage firm and ask questions. Request their literature. Enter your findings in the table. Only after your research is complete should you make your decision. If you are happy with your broker and can form a long-term relationship, your business will benefit, so take your time in making the decision.

Full Service vs. Discount

A full-service broker offers a variety of services not available at a discount brokerage. The concept behind discount brokerages is that they can offer you lower commission fees because you are making your own trading decisions and do not need advice. A full-service brokerage employs people who can make recommendations and give you advice, and they pay these people from your higher commissions. One is not better than the other; you are not limited in the stocks or commodities you can buy through a discounter. The main difference is whether you want to pay for advice or not.

Brokerage Commissions and Fees

Brokerage fees are *not* the most important components in your decision process. Don't get me wrong; they certainly are important but they are not the most important factor. If you negotiate a low commission structure and you get bad fills, you'll be much worse off than if you have average commissions and get good fills.

SETTING UP YOUR ACCOUNT

Once you have completed your research into brokerage commissions, you will ask the brokerage firm you have chosen to send you all the necessary forms for opening a new account. Fill them out carefully, keep a copy for yourself, and send them back to the broker with your deposit to open the account. When they have established the account, usually in just a few days, they will call you back or e-mail you with a password to use, with an account number, and with a phone number to call to make your trades.

The amount of your opening deposit will be governed by the level at which you will be trading. For instance, if you are going to be trading stocks in lots of 100, and the stocks on average cost $50 per share, the minimum you should put in the account would be $5,000. However, if your first trade is a loss (and Murphy's law says it should be), you will need to put more money in the account immediately to cover the loss. As a rule of thumb, I put twice the required minimum in the account. In this case then, you would put $10,000 in the account. In the case of futures trading, where you are using a lot of leverage, you should open the account with twice the required margin.

MARGIN REQUIREMENTS

In practice, stocks typically can be purchased on 50 percent margin. If you want to purchase $10,000 worth of stock, you can do it with $5,000 cash. The requirements for you to do this vary with brokerage houses, so check with your broker first.

Margin requirements for futures contracts vary with the volatility of the market and also differ among commodities. In 1985, the margin for the S&P 500 futures contract was $6,500. By October 1987, the margin had increased to $22,000 per contract. Now, in 2000, the margin for the same contract is at $12,000.

ENTERING YOUR FIRST TRADE

Your first trade is probably the most scary one you will ever face. After spending months in research and paper trading, you will be eager to make that first trade, but if you are like me, you will be very nervous about it. When it's real money, and it is yours, you will gain a lot more respect for the process.

If you are trading electronically, check your order carefully before entering the trade. If you are trading to a futures pit, speak clearly and distinctly and tell the person on the other end of the line only what he or she needs to know to place your order. And, above all, follow your system.

ORDER TYPES

Market orders are not the only type of order you can enter. There are many types of orders, but not all markets accept all types of orders. Ask your broker what types of orders are accepted.

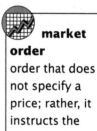 **market order**
order that does not specify a price; rather, it instructs the filling broker to execute the order at the best price available on receipt.

For your reference, here's a list of order types:

cancel
cancel and replace
disregard tape (DRT)
limit
limit on close
market
market if touched (MIT)
market on close (MOC)
market on open only (OO)
or better close only
order cancels order (OCO)
spread
stops
stop close only (SCO)
stop limit
stop limit close only (SLCO)
stop with a limit of _____

These terms do not always mean the same thing in different settings. Your broker can tell you which order types are accepted and give you the meanings of the terms accepted.

LEGAL AND TAX QUESTIONS

Do not invest or trade for the tax man. By that I mean, if you consider the tax consequences of a transaction before you consider the profit potential and risk-reward ratio, then you are investing for the tax man. Taxes do not matter. Would you rather make 10 percent tax-free on an investment—or 100 percent and have to pay taxes?

The more money you make, the more taxes you get to pay. That is a good thing. It just means you are making more money.

Consult with your tax accountant or tax attorney about your individual situation.

ATTORNEYS

You may or may not need an attorney before you start trading. Only you will know that. If you are trading only for your own account and do not take money from anyone else, chances are you do not need an attorney for your trading. If, on the other hand, you are considering managing money for friends or clients, you definitely will need an attorney. Legal advice is well beyond the scope of this book. If you think there is any reason you might need an attorney, consult the one(s) you already employ or look in the yellow pages of the *Traders' Catalog and Resource Guide* and start calling around.

BOOKS

There is not a lot written about the business aspects of trading. The one book that comes to mind is *Trading Is a Business* by Joe Ross. Beyond that, general business management books and business planning books will help point you in the right direction.

REGULATORS

Again, if you trade only for your own account, you probably do not need to worry about regulators. Regulators are there to protect the unsuspecting public from you. If you begin advertising your successes and inviting the public to let you manage their money, then you will be subject to the regulations of the organization that oversees the type of trading you will be doing. There are regulators for futures trading, options trading, stock trading, and so on.

Here are some of the numbers you will need to call. Ask for their literature and information about their regulations so you will be safe and not sorry. Also you can check their websites for information.

Commodity Futures Trading Commission	(202) 254-8630	www.cftc.gov
Nasdaq, Inc.	(202) 728-8000	www.nasdaq.com
National Association of Securities Dealers	(312) 899-4400	www.nasd.com
National Futures Association	(312) 781-1372	www.nfa.futures.org
Securites & Exchange Commission	(202) 942-0020	www.sec.gov

Chapter

Discipline

___

I am a mathematician, not a psychologist. For this reason I asked a prominent traders' coach to pen much of this chapter. Adrienne Laris Toghraie, (adtoghraie@aol.com) author of *Trading on Target*, was kind enough to donate her insight and experience to this effort.

FOLLOWING YOUR SYSTEM

Every successful trader will agree: If you are not disciplined enough to follow the rules you have set up, you will never be successful as a trader.

However, discipline is not a character trait you can wish into existence just because you want to be successful. To be disciplined, you must possess three key psychological elements:

1. Motivation
2. Commitment
3. Persistence

Developing these traits is an ongoing process for most of us. We attend motivational seminars; we take classes; we go to trade shows and retreats—all to hone our skills and replenish our psychological strengths. Trading is a constant process of education and research.

Motivation

You must be driven by passion in order to overcome the procrastination that most people feel when beginning any new venture. Passion is an intensity of feeling that narrows your focus and consolidates your energy toward a single goal.

Passion is the energy that propels you into immediate action. The same level of dedication and energy that is required to become a surgeon, a lawyer, or an astronaut is required to become a professional trader.

Every individual is motivated by a unique set of triggers. What works for one person may not work for another. For that reason, research in the field of personal motivation has demonstrated that you already have all it takes: You do not need someone else to do it for you. To recognize your own motivational model, remember the times in your life when you completed a difficult task or reached a goal because you were passionately motivated. Having identified these past successful achievements, model your current behavior accordingly.

Modeling simply means copying success. To create high achievement for yourself, model your actions after your own previous successes or the successes of others.

Commitment

All achievement requires commitment. The bigger the goal, the higher the level of commitment required. A commitment is a promise you make to yourself. When you have the goal of becoming a trader, each task you complete toward that goal builds trust. When commitments are broken, the unconscious mind will not support us in keeping our agreements. Therefore, it is essential to build a pattern of trust between you and yourself when you are in the development stage. You build this trust pattern by completing each task within your agreed time frame.

A strategy for learning how to keep commitments is to set small achievable tasks and complete them. Doing so provides a pattern of biological feedback for your neurology to follow. Attaching a small reward that makes you feel good is an excellent way to anchor task achievement. Several task achievements in a row will lead to a goal achievement. This positive pattern is the foundation necessary to follow your own rules. This, in and of itself, is a major accomplishment for all traders and is the basis for success.

Most people make commitments before they understand the trade-offs attached to those commitments. It takes sacrifice, investment of time and resources, and facing psychological challenges to become a professional trader. Sacrifice does not mean neglecting everything and everyone else in your life, however. You must balance all areas of your life, or you will create a breeding ground for self-sabotage. Self-sabotage is the worst trap a trader (or anyone else) can fall into, because those who fall sometimes never recover.

Persistence

Studying to be a trader can be a very lonely process. Many traders feel they are not traders until they actually make that first trade. It is important for your motivation to have the attitude that you are a trader once you have made the commitment and that each step is an important part of the process for success. When you choose the right actions in the developmental stage, you will eliminate many of the psychological struggles traders go through when they begin to trade.

It is essential that you not give up too early. Persistence means continuing in the face of opposition. For every good idea you have that actually profits in the market, you will have 99 ideas that fail. It is persistence that differentiates long-term successful traders from the other 80 percent who give up.

KEEPING A DIARY

It is essential for you as a trader to know your daily, weekly, and monthly achievements. Maintaining a log of your accomplishments will document the progress you have made. Doing so is important so that you can celebrate your progress rather than falling into the mind trap of believing that you have accomplished little.

It is also important that you keep a careful and precise diary of events in the market, so that you can later form conclusions from the data. To this day, Joe Granville keeps a daily diary of trading!

Your diary reveals that certain types of economic reports generate fear and therefore down days in the market. You can conclude that the market has specific characteristics at specific times of day. You can analyze the behavior of your system from your diary as well.

WHAT IS BETWEEN YOU AND FOLLOWING YOUR RULES?

You can face many psychological pitfalls when you start to trade your system. Trading is the performance of all the best and worst parts of your psychology. Some of the psychological challenges that traders must conquer when trying to follow their systems are:

- ✔ Emotions
- ✔ Conflicts
- ✔ Attitudes
- ✔ Beliefs

Emotions

Fear is the major emotion that holds most traders back. You must have preparedness in your trading plan. Then you must satisfy the needs of the part of you that is afraid to take the correct trading actions; for example, if you are afraid to enter the markets, perhaps you should have someone else initiate the trade.

Conflicts

First, you must recognize the conflicts you have within yourself—perhaps part of you is afraid to take risk and part of you knows it should stick to your money management rules. Negotiate between these two parts of yourself to come up with an amicable working relationship.

Attitudes

Reframe your negative attitudes! A common negative attitude that traders share is "It is a losing day if I lose money." Transform this negative attitude thus: "It is a losing day only if I do not follow my system and learn the lessons the market is teaching me." All traders experience drawdown. It is part of doing business.

Beliefs

Your beliefs are what is true for you. It is important to notice what you believe about yourself as a successful trader, what you believe about your system, and what you believe about making money. Beliefs direct our neurology to the kind of action that manifests our getting what we believe in. ("Be careful what you ask for, you might get it.")

If you have negative beliefs about becoming a successful trader, change this by beginning to dwell on what positive beliefs would be more useful, until they stir you into positive feelings. ("What you think about you bring about.") For instance, if you are thinking "I can never be a top trader," transform your thoughts to "If I do all the things a top trader does, I will be a top trader."

COACHES AND PSYCHOLOGISTS

The foregoing is a brief overview (by Adrienne Toghraie), of some of the psychological challenges that can face you as a trader. Entire books are devoted to these subjects, specifically for traders. Seminars and workshops focus on the psychology of trading.

Accomplished traders all agree that conquering the psychological aspects makes all the difference in attaining positive trading results.

This is easier said than done. While you cannot have trust and discipline without a proven trading system or methodology, the best system in the world will do you no good if you do not have the discipline to follow it. These two elements go hand in hand.

You do not hesitate to take golf lessons or dance lessons or classes about someone's system of trading; so do not hesitate to take lessons on the psychological aspects of trading. Professional help can save you from considerable unnecessary losses. To be successful all you have to do is monitor your performance, be honest with yourself, and take the right actions.

WHO YOU GONNA CALL?

Coaches and psychologists who deal specifically with the financial community do more than counsel you through difficult emotional times. These specialists offer motivational training, audiotapes, videotapes, literature, and seminars in addition to telephone and personal consulting.

Charles Faulkner
Mental Edge Trading Associates
141 W Jackson Drive, Suite 278
Chicago, IL 60604
(800) 500-7657   fax (800) 500-7657

Dr. Richard McCall
Misogi International
PO Box 23413
Little Rock, AR 72221
(800) 336-7061   fax (501) 568-8157

Adrienne Toghraie
Trading on Target
100 Lavewood Lane
Cary, NC 27511
(919) 851-8288   fax (919) 851-9979

Van K. Tharp
Van Tharp Associates
8308 Belgium Street
Raleigh, NC 27606
(919) 362-5591   fax (919) 362-6020

Chapter 18

Evaluating Your Performance

At the very least, you must know the profit or loss of each trade you make. Keeping a running total of your profits and losses keeps you honest. Gamblers talk about their big wins, but they never tell you about their losses. Trading is not gambling, it is a profession, so keep good books.

For every trade you make, you must record the price at which you entered the trade and the price at which you exit. From these two numbers you compute your *profit* or loss.

If your trade was long—that is, you bought and then sold in that order—then your profit is calculated as:

Profit = Exit Price – Entry Price

If your trade was short—that is, you sold and then bought in that order—then your profit is calculated as:

Profit = Entry Price – Exit Price

I cannot stress to you strongly enough: Keep good books. I don't care whether you use plain paper and a pen, green ledger paper, or a computer, but keep track of

 profit
difference between the price at which you sell something and the price at which you bought it, less any transaction costs.

everything you do. Otherwise, you are just gambling and you have no statistics that can improve your performance upon which to base subsequent calculations.

See Figure 18.1 for an example of keeping track of your trades in a spreadsheet. This is the very least you must know. But it is not really enough. We math types call this "necessary, but not sufficient." You can keep better statistics than these and thereby have more confidence in your trading.

equity
generic term for ownership interest in an asset.

Your *equity* is the cumulative amount of money you have made or lost trading. In the spreadsheet in Figure 18.1, the equity in column G is calculated by adding all your profits and subtracting all your losses.

The more you know statistically about your trading, the more able you will be to follow it during periods of drawdown. (See Figure 18.2.)

In practice, we measure drawdown from the highest equity high to the lowest equity low. Looking at this number answers the question: "How bad can it be?" What is your worst case?

	A	B	C	D	E	F	G
1	Date	Time	Type	Cts	Price	Entry P/L	Cumulative
2	10/10/01	12:45 PM	Buy	1	$580.70		
3	10/11/01	12:55 PM	LExit	1	$582.65	$945.00	$945.00
4	10/13/01	11:00 AM	Sell	1	$590.40		
5	10/17/01	9:45 AM	SExit	1	$586.50	$1,920.00	$2,865.00

FIGURE 18.1 Keeping your trades in a spreadsheet.

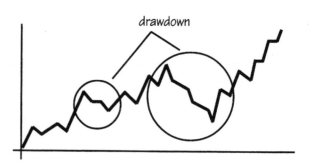

FIGURE 18.2 An equity chart showing periods of drawdown.

USEFUL STATISTICS

In addition to keeping track of your equity and your drawdown, there are several other numbers you should compute. Many of the financial software products will calculate these statistics automatically for you as part of their portfolio modules.

Figure 18.3 gives an example of the information available from a Performance Summary from *TradeStation* by Omega Research.

Study the information in Figure 18.3. There is a lot to be learned. The total net profit is not the most important number. We know from Chapter 15 that if the system is profitable (has a positive mathematical expectation) we can maximize the profit through money management; so as long as the total net profit is positive, we can improve it.

The first thing I look at in this figure is the *largest winning trade*. If the largest winning trade accounts for most of the profit, then the system probably will not continue to work over time. I like to see profits accumulate a little bit at a time, which shows me that the system wins in a variety of market environments.

Second, I look at the *number of trades* and the size of the *average trade*. With 20 trades, as opposed to two or three trades, we know we have made enough trades to begin evaluating the system's behavior. We know from the

Performance Summary: All Trades			
Total net profit	$ 6,275	Open position P/L	$ 2,425
Gross profit	$13,720	Gross loss	$ -7,445
Total # of trades	20	•Percent profitable	55%
Number winning trades	11	Number losing trades	9
Largest winning trade	$ 2,870	Largest losing trade	$ -2,255
Average winning trade	$1,247	Average losing trade	$ -827
▸ Ratio avg win/avg loss	1.51	· Avg trade (win & loss)	$314
Max consec. winners	5	Max consec. losers	3
Avg # bars in winners	26	Avg # bars in losers	8
Max intraday drawdown	$ -3,315		
Profit factor	1.84	Max # contracts held	1
Account size required	$ 15,315	Return on account	41%

FIGURE 18.3 Performance summary.

size of the average trade that we are making enough money to get in and out of the trade and account for slippage and the time it takes actually to enter the trade in the market.

Professional traders can make a good living with systems that show 40 percent or more profitable trades, as long as the *ratio of the average win to average loss* is high enough to generate a positive mathematical expectation. Since Figure 18.3 shows that 55 percent of the trades are profitable, that is acceptable. We calculate that number by taking the total number of winning trades (11) and dividing by the total number of trades (20).

Finally I look at the *maximum consecutive losers* and the average number of bars (whether daily, weekly, or hourly) in losers to see whether my emotional makeup and personality can stand the heat in this kitchen. Looking at the figure again, there are three losers in a row before encountering a winning trade. That is not too bad emotionally. And there are only eight bars, on average, in each losing trade while the winners, on average, last for 26 bars. I think I can handle that.

Other programs provide additional trade information, such as how many times your stop was hit, total commission expenses, maximum equity drop, maximum trade drawdown, margin interest expenses, interest earned, and commission-to-equity ratio.

An important component of any trading software is the ability to display a chart of your equity. Since these programs are always graphically oriented, and a chart is worth a thousand numbers, it only makes sense to be able to visually inspect the progress of your trading. Professional traders use other statistics to monitor the success (or failure) of their trading. When you get to that point, a good book to study is *Managed Futures in the Institutional Portfolio* by Charles B. Epstein, where you can find coverage of such topics as *standard deviation,* Sharpe ratio, *Sterling ratio, maximum drawdown,* recovery time, risk, and risk of ruin.

If you decide to diversify and trade more than one system, or more than one instrument (i.e., stocks and sugar futures), then you need to know whether the sys-

standard deviation
the positive square root of the expected value of the square of the difference between a random variable and its mean. The dispersion of observations from the mean observation. This measure often is expressed as a percentage on an annualized basis.

Sterling ratio (or return to drawdown or MAR ratio)
ratio that compares the rate of return with the worst-case loss, thus a measurement or risk-adjusted rate of return, calculated as: (Annual ROR)/(Maximum drawdown).

tems are correlated. If two systems produce essentially the same results, they are said to be highly correlated; if two systems are opposite each other (one wins when the other loses and vice versa), they are not correlated (or, are negatively correlated). Depending on the profitability of the systems, two noncorrelated techniques could conceivably eliminate drawdown periods by covering for each other. One is winning while the other is losing.

If two systems are highly correlated, then would you trade them both? In that situation you would be winning twice as fast, but you also would be losing twice as fast.

For these reasons, it is important to determine the correlation coefficient to multiple trading systems before you trade them together.

The formula and explanation of this procedure can be found in Chuck Epstein's book *Managed Futures in the Institutional Portfolio.*

In his books, Ralph Vince covers valuable concepts that are *musts* for the serious evaluation of your performance. Before you devote yourself to following your system religiously, run your hypothetical trades through a few of Vince's exercises. Either you'll discard your system as unworkable or you will gain great insight into how to maximize your system's profits. The books by Vince to date are: *The Mathematics of Money Management, Portfolio Management Formulas,* and *The New Money Management.*

maximum drawdown (or largest cumulative decline) largest cumulative percentage (peak-to-valley) decline in capital of a trading account or portfolio. This measurement of risk identifies the worst-case scenario for a managed futures investment within a time period.

Back-Office Details

What the heck is a back office? you say! You do not even have a front office. Well, in trading terminology, "back office" means the stuff that goes on behind the scenes. Your system and the events of actually trading are front-office tasks. The paperwork part, where you keep track of each and every detail about your individual trades, their statistics, the account balance, your checking account, how much you spend on office supplies . . . that's back-office information.

If you are a small-time operator, keeping your logs and running balance on a piece of grid paper or ledger paper may be good enough. When I first began trading, I kept these details in a spreadsheet.

As time goes on and your profits grow, your business naturally will expand. At some point the spreadsheet method will not be enough. You will have so many trades and formulas in the spreadsheet that you start losing track of things. Producing the summary reports you want will become difficult. When that happens, you should consider using a software program designed for back-office accounting, or you might consider using a professional accounting firm that specializes in back-office accounting for traders.

ACCOUNTING

Do It Yourself?

Doing it yourself with an accounting program designed for traders presents two immediate advantages: You are in control of your documentation, and you will gain insight into your system's successes and failures. Often the process of documenting your trades will cause you to think of ways to improve the results, as you begin to recognize patterns to your profits and losses.

Several companies offer back-office accounting software for traders:

Advent Software, Inc.	(800) 727-0605
Allied Financial Services	(800) 831-7636
Atis International, Inc.	(312) 527-2847
Austin Associates	(419) 841-8521
Comprehensive Software Systems	(303) 526-5515
Financial Models Company	(312) 345-0045
ITS Associates, Inc.	(617) 528-7800
Orbit Software	(402) 498-5712
Plaid Brothers Software	(800) IC-PLAID
Princeton Financial Systems	(609) 987-2400
Synergy Software Solutions	44 (0) 1582 424282
Tech Hackers	(212) 344-9500
Thompson Financial	(617) 856-2700
TradeManage LLC	(201) 791-6475
Xenomorph	44 (0)20 8971 0080

You can even use accounting programs like Quicken to keep track of your trading, depending on what you are trading. Quicken can keep track of stocks, bonds, mutual funds, Real Estate Investment Trusts and partnerships, Individual Retirement and/or Keogh accounts, variable annuities, money market funds, certificates of deposit or Treasury bills, real estate, and retirement plans.

As with all your research, as you become interested in purchasing software to keep track of your trading, call each of the vendors, get their literature and demo disk, make a table of pros and cons, and evaluate each package before making a purchase.

Accountants

In my computer database I list hundreds of accountants who work with traders. I cannot possibly list them all here; refer to the *Traders' Catalog & Resource Guide* and/or the Money Mentor (www.moneymentor.com). Understand that not all accountants are versed in the whys and wherefores of trading. Your income tax accountant is not necessarily the person who can administer your trading records. Specialized accountants stay on top of regulations that restrict and govern trading and can give you hints about some of the best strategies for minimizing your tax liability.

Complete Back Office Services

A number of firms offer a package of complete services that frees you from assuming the role of clerk and accountant and lets you focus on your trading methods. While these services are usually expensive, if you become a frequent or large trader (that's the goal, isn't it?), you may need to hire one. Again, I keep the list up to date in other media, but you might want to contact:

Acceltek Accounting Systems	(773) 804-0074
Commodity Compliance Services, Inc.	(800) 445-6535

Legal and Tax Questions

Ted Tesser's *Trader's Tax Solution* is the one book you need to read when it comes to this aspect of trading. Tesser covers everything you need to know and watch out for, including filing under trader status, deductions and expenses, passive vs. investment income, audits, calculating your true investment return after taxes, and "how far can you go."

The tax law with respect to capital gains, allowable expenses, and tax rates changes frequently. Consult your attorney and your tax accountant for advice on these subjects.

Attorneys

Again the list is lengthy and is available in the *Traders' Catalog and Resource Guide* or The Money Mentor. If you need an attorney, be sure to get one who specializes not only in trading endeavors but in the particular aspect of trading with which you need help. I think attorneys specialize in even narrower subspecialties than do physicians.

REGULATORS

Several organizations exist to protect the public from malpractice in the exchanges. Each of these regulating bodies has its own set of guidelines governing what you can and can not do. There are circumstances under which you can trade money for your friends and situations in which you can not. These restrictions change with time, so if you consider trading anyone's money besides your own, be sure to contact one or all of the following agencies:

CFTC—Commodity Futures
Trading Commission www.cftc.gov

The CFTC was established by the Commodity Futures Trading Commissions Act of 1974, along with the National Futures Association. It is an independent agency with exclusive jurisdiction over futures trading.

NFA—National Futures
Association www.nfa.futures.org

NFA is a not-for-profit membership corporation formed in 1976 to become a futures industry's self-regulatory organization under Section 17 of the Commodity Exchange Act.

Nasdaq—National Association of Securities Dealers www.nasdaq.com

An agency that represents securities dealers who trade for themselves in the United States. It is empowered by the U. S. Securities and Exchange Commission to regulate dealers' operations in the over-the-counter markets and has the authority to censure, fine, suspend, or expel members who break its rules.

SEC—Securities and Exchange Commission www.sec.gov

An independent U. S. federal regulatory agency, created by the Securities Exchange Act of 1934, that administers statutes designed to provide the fullest possible disclosure to the investing public and to protect the interests of both the general public and investors against malpractice in the securities and financial markets. The SEC supervises all national securities exchanges and associations, registers all issues of securities offered in interstate commerce or through the mail, registers brokers and dealers who engage in over-the-counter trading, and regulated mutual funds and other investment companies, investment counselors and advisors, and practically all other individuals and firms engaged in the investment business.

Conclusion

There is possibly nothing more satisfying than working for yourself, generating your income your own way. There is also probably nothing more difficult and all consuming.

When you work for yourself or own your own business, you have a full-time job—24 hours a day. There are no vacations, no sick days, and no one else to blame when things go wrong. But you can wear shorts to work if you want to and come and go at your own pace.

STEP BY STEP

I am often asked to provide a checklist for beginners, against which you can measure your progress. Most beginning traders do not want to hear what I am about to say, but they come back to me after they are experienced, acknowledging that this admonition is indeed true.

There are three phases to becoming a successful trader:

Phase One: Think

1. Listen to what others have to say, to the news, to forecasts, to lectures and seminars.

2. Observe the action of the market, its patterns and results.

3. Read everything you can get your hands on.

Phase Two: Test

1. Research.

2. Test your theories with pen, paper, and a calculator.

3. Test your theories in a spreadsheet.

4. Test your theories with analysis software.

5. If your theory merits further investigation, based on the first four steps, run exhaustive tests by thirds. (See Chapter 15.)

6. Develop a system that has a positive mathematical expectation, that pays you an acceptable potential hourly wage, and with which you are comfortable.

Phase Three: Follow

1. *Paper trade.* Without lying to yourself, put on paper (in ink, with time stamps) each and every trade your system calls for.

2. When you are confident that you can follow every signal your system gives, then you may begin actually to enter trades in the market.

3. Do not vary from the rules you have established. If you conclude that you must override your rules at some point, then you have not tested and verified your rules properly. *Do not trade if you cannot follow your system.* Go back to Phase Two and conduct additional research until you have so thoroughly defined and exhaustively tested your rules that you can trade your system almost unconsciously.

Appendix A

Magazines and Newspapers

MAGAZINES

Active Trader
www.activetradermag.com
555 W. Madison, Tower 1
Suite 1210
Chicago, IL 60661
(312) 775-5421

Futures
250 S. Wacker
Chicago, IL 60606
(800) 972-9316

Individual Investor
www.individualinvestor.com
125 Broad Street
New York, NY 10004
(212) 742-2200

Institutional Investor
488 Madison Avenue
New York, NY 10022
(212) 303-3233

Technical Analysis of Stocks and Commodities
4757 California Avenue, SW
Seattle, WA 98116
(800) 832-4642

Traders' Catalog & Resource Guide
2075 Corte del Nogal, Suite C
Carlsbad, CA 92009
(760) 930-1050

Traders World
401 S. LaSalle
Chicago, IL 60605
(312) 347-7805

Wall Street & Technology
(800) 875-9763

NEWSPAPERS

Barron's
PO Box 300
Princeton, NJ 08543
(609) 520-4244

Investor's Business Daily
12655 Beatrice Avenue
Los Angeles, CA 90056
(800) 831-2525

USA Today
100 Wilson Boulevard
Arlington, VA 22229
(800) USA-0001

Wall Street Journal
(800) 451-5200

Software Vendors

AbleSys Corp.	ASCTrend Software	(510) 538-0926
AIQ Inc.	MarketExpert, StockExpert, TradingExpert, OptionsExpert	(702) 831-2999
Aspen Graphics	Aspen Graphics, AspeNet	(970) 945-2921
AustinSoft	OptionTrader 98	(212) 488-9000
Barra, Inc.	portfolio management, risk management	(510) 548-5442
CDA/Wiesenberger	mutual fund tracking software	(301) 975-9600
Commodity Quote Graphics	CQG	(800) 525-7082
Delphi Economics Inc.	Viking 6.1	(201) 867-4303
Deltasoft Financial Technologies Inc.	OptionOracle	(805) 644-2225
Dow Jones Telerate		(800)334-3813
Equis International, Inc.	MetaStock	(801) 265-9996 ×TCRG

Financial Engineering Associates	pricing and risk management	(510) 548-6200
FutureSource		(800) 621-2628
Investors' Technical Services	Behold!	(512) 367-4626
iSoft	StockWiz	(800) 909-4218
Market Communications Group	MarketPro	(800) 810-0111
MarketSoft Research	TradeWind	(800) 495-7638
Masterpiece Software	Free Java and ActiveX Online Charting	(423) 919-8427
Nirvana Systems, Inc.	OmniTrader	(512) 345-2545
North Systems	CandlePower 5, ActionScan	(503) 364-3829
Omega Research	Wall Street Analyst, SuperCharts, TradeStation, OptionStation, RadarScreen	(305) 551-9991 x4228
Pinpoint Strategies Inc.	Investigator 2.0	(650) 938-5266
Stelar International	Professional Trade Advisor	(719) 266-8710
Roberts-Slade Inc.	FirstAlert	(801) 375-6850
RTR Software Inc.	TechniFilter Plus	(919) 856-9600
Small Investor's Software Company	PointsAhead	(516) 598-0218
Strategem Software International	SmarTrader	(504) 885-7353
Technical Tools	ChartBook, QuoteButler	(407) 361-9567
Townsend Analytics, Ltd.	TAL Trading Tools	(312) 621-0141
Trendsetter Software	Personal Hotline, Pro Analyst (MAC)	(714) 547-5005
Window on WallStreet, Inc.	Window on WallStreet Pro 5.0	(972) 783-6792

Glossary

account executive (AE) person who is in charge of a brokerage account.

advance-decline line each day's number of declining issues is subtracted from the number of advancing issues. The net difference is added to a running sum, if the difference is positive, or subtracted from the running sum, if the difference is negative, charted as a single line.

annuity a contract where the buyer (annuitant) pays a sum of money to receive regular payments for life or for a fixed period of time.

arbitrage simultaneous purchase and sale of two different but closely related items to take advantage of a disparity in their prices.

arms equivolume a charting method, developed by Richard Arms, wherein the width of the body represents the day's volume, while the vertical height represents the price. Simply stated, the wider the body, the greater the volume.

arms index see *TRIN*.

artificial intelligence field of computer science dedicated to producing programs that attempt to mimic the processes of the human brain.

ask an offer to sell something at a specified price. The asking price is the lowest price at which any seller is prepared to sell.

associated person (AP) individual who solicits orders, customers, or customer funds (or who supervises persons so engaged) on behalf of a Futures Commission Merchant (FCM), Introducing Broker (IB), or Commodities Trading Advisor (CTA).

at-the-money option whose strike price is nearest the current price of the underlying deliverable.

auction method for selling an asset to the highest bidder.

average annual return rate of return that, if compounded over the duration of the track record, would yield the cumulative gain or loss actually produced during that period.

average directional movement index (ADX) technical indicator, developed by J. Welles Wilder, that measures a market's trend intensity.

back-end load fee paid when withdrawing money from a fund.

back month contract month with the farthest expiration in the future, as opposed to the spot, or current month.

back office operations of a trading organization that do not deal directly with the process of buying and selling securities.

back-testing process of testing a trading strategy on historical data.

bankers' acceptances (BAs) short-term, non–interest-bearing notes sold at a discount and redeemed at maturity for full face value. Primarily used to finance foreign trade.

bar used on charts to plot a single time period and its constituent high, low, open, and close.

bar chart type of chart constructed out of bars that reflect the price information in a specified time period.

basis difference between the price of futures and the spot price.

basis point term used to describe amount of change in yield. One hundred basis points equals 1 percent.

bear market sustained period of falling stock prices usually preceding or accompanied by a period of poor economic performance known as a recession. The opposite of a bull market.

beta term used to describe the price volatility of securities. Standard & Poor's 500 index is assigned a beta of 1. Anything with a beta above 1 is considered to be more volatile than the index; anything below 1 has less volatility than the S&P 500 index.

bid offer to purchase something at a specified price. The bid price is the highest price any buyer is prepared to pay.

bond long-term promissory note that obligates the borrower to make specified payments over a specific period of time.

boolean variable that may have one of only two possible values: true or false. After George Boole, English logician, credited with the invention of Boolean logic.

bounce reversal of a downtrend at a point of resistance.

box the area of a point-and-figure chart into which the technician places one X or O, representing a given amount of price increase or decrease represented by a box on a point-and-figure chart.

break very fast drop in price.

breakaway gap movement of price into a new range that leaves an area on a chart at which no trading occurred.

breakeven analysis calculation of the approximate sales volume required to just cover costs, below which production would be unprofitable and above which it would be profitable. Breakeven analysis focuses on the relationship between fixed cost, variable cost, and profit.

breakout point when the market price moves out of the trend channel.

bull market stock market that is characterized by rising prices over a long period of time. The time span is not precise, but it represents a period of investor optimism, lower interest rates, and economic growth. The opposite of a bear market.

byte single character of computer memory or storage.

call market preopening consensus as to what the opening prices may be.

call option contract that gives the buyer of the option the right, but not the obligation, to take delivery of the underlying security at a specific price within a certain time.

call price price of a call option.

cancel (or straight cancel) instruction to disregard an order that you previously entered but no longer want.

cancel/replace instructs the broker to cancel an existing order and place instead a new order that has adjustments made in the price, action, quantity, and/or duration. You may not change the month or commodity in a cancel/replace.

candlestick charts charting method, originally from Japan, in which the high and low are plotted as a single line and are referred to as shadows. The price range between the open and the close is plotted as a narrow rectangle and is referred to as the body. If the close is above the open, the body is white. If the close is below the open, the body is black.

Chaikin oscillator created by subtracting a 10-day EMA (Exponential Moving Average) from a three-day EMA of the accumulation/distribution line.

channel in charting, a price channel contains prices throughout a trend. There are three basic ways to draw channels: parallel, rounded, and those that connect highs or lows.

clearing house adjunct to a futures exchange, through which transactions executed on the floor of the exchange are settled, using a process of matching purchases and sales.

clearing member member of the clearing house. Each clearing member also must be a member of the exchange. Each member of the exchange, however, need not be a member of the clearing association.

commission amount of money paid to a broker for a transaction.

commodity pool operator (CPO) individual or organization that operates or solicits funds for a commodity pool.

commodity trading advisor (CTA) individual or organization that, for compensation or profit, directly or indirectly advises others as to the value or the advisability of buying or selling futures contracts or commodity options.

continuous data one long price series of data that never expires. When a current commodity month expires, the ending prices are spliced to the next front-month contract and adjustments are made to the entire series of data based on the gap between the current contract and the front month. While in theory these data can be used for historical back-testing of systems, it is likely that no trades ever actually took place at these prices.

contract standardized agreement that, because of its uniformity, makes the buying and selling of its obligations easier and more liquid.

contrary investing investing against the prevailing wisdom.

convergence coming together of prices and/or indicators.

correction any price reaction within the market leading to an adjustment by as much as one-third to two-thirds of the previous gain.

coupon interest that is paid on a regular basis to the owner of a bond or debt security.

cover purchasing back a contract that was sold earlier.

curve-fitting development of a set of complex mathematical or procedural rules that most closely approximate the known data or conditions.

cycle repetitive pattern in price or time.

day order order that is to be executed, if possible, during one day only. If the order cannot be filled during the day specified, it is automatically canceled at the close.

day trading establishing and liquidating positions within one day's trading.

delayed data continuously updated price and volume information that lags real-time data by a specific interval.

derivative financial contract that does not necessarily have value of its own but whose perceived value is based on the value of the underlying instrument(s).

discretionary account account for which buying and selling orders can be placed at the discretion of the broker or other designated person, without the prior consent of the account owner. The account owner signs a prior agreement granting the designated person or broker the power of attorney to place such trades.

disregard tape (DRT) market order that gives the floor broker the discretion to delay the execution of a market order if he or she believes the order can be executed at a better price by so doing. DRT orders are accepted on a "not held" basis only.

divergence parting or deviation of prices and/or indicators. In technical analysis, the term often is used to mean that technical indicators fail to corroborate or confirm one another.

diversification minimizing risk by investing in a wide range of securities.

dividend share of a company's net profits distributed by the company to a class of its stock holders.

drawdown reduction in account equity as a result of a trade or series of trades.

Durbin-Watson statistic (DWS) probability that first order correlation exists. With a range of 0 to 4, the closer the DWS is to 2.0, the lower the probability is.

efficient market theory theory that all known information is already discounted by the market and reflected in the price due to market participants acting on the information.

Elliott Wave Theory pattern recognition technique, published by Ralph N. Elliott in 1939, that holds that the stock market follows a rhythm or pattern of five waves up with three waves down in a bull market and five waves down with three waves up in a bear market to form a complete cycle of eight waves.

end-of-day data data based on the closing price for the day. Often these data contain the open, high, and low for the day as well.

envelope lines surrounding an index or indicator—that is, trading bands.

equity generic term for ownership interest in an asset.

Eurodollar dollars deposited in foreign banks, with the futures contract reflecting the rates offered between London branches of top U. S. banks and foreign banks.

exchange association of persons engaged in the business of buying and selling stocks, futures, and/or options.

ex-dividend date date on which stock is sold without dividend. Under the five-day delivery plan, buyers of the stock on the fourth business day preceding the stockholder-of-record date will not receive the declared dividend.

exercise price amount for which shares can be bought or sold under the option. Also known as the strike price.

expected months to new peak average number of months between any randomly selected peak month and the subsequent month when the cumulative return will exceed the cumulative return for the selected peak month. This measure relates to futures events but is based on historical data.

expert systems dynamic but not adaptable. They are rule-driven systems that cannot learn as the result of new information being fed into the systems.

expiration last day on which an option can be exercised.

exponential moving average (EMA) EMA for day i is calculated as: $A_i = \alpha P_i + (1 - \alpha)(A_i - 1)$, where P is the price on day i and α (alpha) is a smoothing constant ($0 < \alpha < i$). Alpha may be estimated as $2/(n + 1)$, where n is the length of the simple moving average.

fade selling a rising price or buying a falling price. For example, a trader fading an up opening would be short.

fair value theoretical price generated by an option pricing model such as Black-Scholes.

fast Fourier transform method by which to decompose data into a sum of sinusoids of varying cycle length, with each cycle being a fraction of a common fundamental cycle length.

Federal Reserve the seven member board that establishes monetary policy (interest rates, credit, etc.) and monitors the economic health of the country.

fill an executed order; sometimes the term refers to the price at which an order is executed.

fill or kill (FOK) order, that instructs a broker to bid (to buy) or offer (to sell) at a specified price (which should be at or near the current market) and to cancel the order immediately if it is unable to be filled.

floor broker (FB) individual who executes any orders for the purchase or sale of any commodity futures or options contract on any contract market for any other person.

floor trader (FT) individual who executes trades for the purchase or sale of any commodity futures or options contract on any contract market for his or her own account. Also known as a local.

forward testing strategy of testing a fully optimized system to see if it works on fresh data.

front-end load sales charge for buying into a mutual fund. The sales charge typically can run as high as 4.0 to 8.5 percent and legally can be 9.0 percent or more.

front month the closest month. For instance, if a futures contract expires quarterly (March, June, September, and December) and it is currently August, the front month is September.

front office operations of a trading organization that deal directly with the process of buying and selling securities.

fundamental analysis analytical method by which only the sales, earnings, and value of a given tradable's assets may be considered. This theory holds that stock market activity may be predicted by looking at the relative data and statistics of a stock as well as the management of the company in question and its earnings.

futures investment contracts which specify the quantity and price of a commodity to be purchased or sold at a later, specified date.

futures commission merchant (FCM) individual or organization that does both of the following: (1) solicits or accepts orders to buy or sell futures contracts or commodity options and (2) accepts money or other assets from customers to support such orders.

fuzzy logic problem-solving method that processes inexact information inexactly.

gap time period in which the range is completely above or below the previous time period's range.

head and shoulders chart pattern often interpreted to mean a trend reversal may be imminent. A head-and-shoulder pattern often is associated with the topping of a market; an inverted head and shoulders is associated with the bottoming of a market. The neckline is the resistance or support area in the formation. The pattern also can be used to project prices by measuring the distance between the neckline and the head and adding that distance to the direction of the breakout, if one occurs.

hypothetical trade any trade not actually executed for an account.

index statistical composite that measures changes in the economy or in financial markets, can be expressed in percent changes from a base year or from the previous time period. Most common are the S&P 500 and the Dow Jones Industrial Average.

in the money call option whose strike price is lower than the stock or future's price, or a put option whose strike price is higher than the underlying stock or future's price.

intrinsic value portion of an option's premium represented when the cash market price is greater than the exercise price.

introducing broker (IB) individual or organization that solicits or accepts orders to buy or sell futures contracts or commodity options but does not accept money or other assets from customers to support such orders.

Japanese candlestick charting method, originally from Japan, in which the high and low are plotted as a single line and are referred to as shadows. The price range between the open and the close is plotted as a narrow rectangle and is referred to as the body. If the close is above the open, the body is white. If the close is below the open, the body is black.

lag number of data points that a filter, such as a moving average, follows or trails the input price data.

leverage use of borrowed money with invested funds to increase returns. The effect is to magnify profits or losses and increase the amount of risk.

limit price that the filling broker must equal or better in the execution of your order.

limit order order to buy or sell when a trade in the market occurs at a predetermined price.

limit up, limit down exchange restrictions on the maximum upward or downward movement permitted in the price for a commodity during any trading session.

line chart type of chart that is similar to the scatter chart but connects the adjacent dots with a straight line.

liquidity ability of an asset to be converted into cash quickly and without any price discount.

load that portion of the offering price that goes toward selling costs such as sales commissions and distribution.

local also called a floor trader; a member of an exchange who generally trades only for his or her own account or for an account he or she controls.

locked limit market that, if not restricted, would seek price equilibrium outside the limit but instead moves to the limit and ceases to trade.

long state of actually owning a security, contract, or commodity.

MACD (moving average convergence divergence) difference between two exponentially smoothed moving averages of different length (often 12 and 24 period). Technicians often use the crossing of this value over the zero line to signal buying or selling opportunities.

management fee amount paid to the administrator and/or management company (who may also serve as an investment advisor) for services rendered to the fund and included in the expense ratio.

margin in stock trading, an account in which purchase of stock may be financed with borrowed money; in futures trading, the deposit placed with the clearing house to assure fulfillment of the contract. This amount varies with market volatility and is settled in cash.

margin call demand by the lender of a margin loan that the borrower repay all or a portion of the loan.

market 1. an order that is executed immediately, at the best available price. 2. a public place where buyers and sellers make transactions, directly or via intermediaries.

market if touched (MIT) order that becomes a market order if and when the market hits a price you specify. Like limit orders, buy MITs are entered at or below the current market and sell MITs and entered at or above the current price. Unlike limit orders, there are no limitations placed on the floor broker as to fill price; the broker will execute the order at the best available price, the same as any market order.

market maker brokerage or bank that maintains a firm bid and ask price in a given security by standing ready, willing, and able to buy or sell at publicly quoted prices.

market on close (MOC) market order that can be filled only within the closing range.

market on open only (OO) market order that must be executed within the official opening range of prices.

market order order that does not specify a price; rather, it instructs the filling broker to execute the order at the best price available on receipt.

mathematical expectation $[(1 + A) \times P] - 1$, where P = Probability of winning, and A = (amount you can win)/(amount you can lose).

maximum adverse excursion historical measure by which closed winning trades have gone against you.

maximum drawdown (or largest cumulative decline) largest cumulative percentage (peak-to-valley) decline in capital of a trading account or portfolio. This measurement of risk identifies the worst-case scenario for a managed futures investment within a time period.

MB abbreviation for megabyte. A megabyte is 1,024 kilobytes, or roughly 1 million bytes.

McClellan Oscillator index based on the New York Stock Exchange net advances divided by net declines, providing a measure of such conditions as overbought/oversold and market direction on a short-to-intermediate term basis.

momentum time series representing change of today's price from some fixed number of days back in history.

moving average mathematical transform that is the sum of the current value plus $(n-1)$ previous values divided by n. The result smooths fluctuations in the raw data.

moving average convergence-divergence (MACD) technical analysis term for the crossing of two exponentially smoothed moving averages.

multiple linear regression more than one independent variable is used to account for the variability in one dependent variable.

mutual fund investment company that continually offers new shares and stands ready to redeem existing shares from the owners.

net asset value (NAV) total market value of an investment company's shares—securities, cash, and any accrued earnings—minus its liabilities, divided by the number of shares outstanding.

not held order that a broker will fill at whatever price is available, not necessarily at your price. Often this occurs during fast market conditions.

odd lot order of shares that is not a multiple of 100.

on-balance volume technical indicator consisting of a single continuous line that represents buying or selling pressure.

optimization finding the best or most favorable conditions or parameters.

option contract that gives the buyer the right (but not the obligation) to buy or sell a given security at a given price by some specified time in the future.

options expiration third Friday of the month shown.

or better close only limit order valid only during the closing range.

order cancels order (OCO) also called one cancels the other. This order consists of two separate buy or sell instructions to the filling broker, who will execute whichever portion of the order he or she is able to do first and then automatically cancel the alternate instruction.

out of the money condition of a call option or warrant when the price of the underlying investment is lower than the striking price. The condition of a put option when the striking price is lower than the price of the underlying investment.

outlier value removed from the other values to such an extreme that its presence cannot be attributed to the random combination of chance causes.

overbought/oversold indicator indicator that attempts to define when prices have moved too far and too fast in either direction and thus are vulnerable to a reaction.

overfitting parameters of a trading system are selected to return the single highest profit over the historical data, often resulting in a system that works only on this exact data set.

over the counter nationwide network of brokers/dealers who buy and sell securities that, for the most part, are not listed on an exchange.

paper trade to make simulated transactions with now real money, to practice or test theories.

par full principal amount of an investment instrument.

parameter variable, set of data, or rule that establishes a precise format for a model.

pit a specially constructed arena (usually circular) on the trading floor of exchanges where trading is conducted. Some exchanges call these area rings rather than pits.

point and figure type of chart that plots price moves without regard to time. Each column represents a move and continues until the move is reversed and a new column starts.

premium price a buyer pays to an option writer for granting an option contract.

profit difference between the price at which you sell something and the price at which you bought it, less any transaction costs.

program trading trades based on signals from computer programs, usually entered directly from the trader's computer to the market's computer system. Since 1987 program trading is limited to times when the market is not volatile. For instance, there is a 50-point collar on the Dow Jones Industrial Average, so that no program trades may take place if the average moves beyond this limit up or down in a single day's trading.

price/earnings ratio (PE) price of the stock, divided by earnings per share reported over the last four quarters.

put option the right, but not the obligation, to sell shares at the exercise price on or before the expiration date.

put price price of a put option.

range high and low transaction prices of a given security during a given period.

rate of return according to Commodity Futures Trading Commission Regulation 4.21 (a)(4)(ii)(F), rate of return is calculated by dividing the net performance for the month or quarter by the net asset value at the beginning of the period.

real-time data data regarding bid, ask, time, and sales, that are transmitted as they happen.

relative strength index indicator invented by J. Welles Wilder and used to ascertain overbought/oversold and divergent situations.

repurchase agreement (repo) financial transaction in which one party purchases securities for cash and a second party simultaneously agrees to buy them back in the future at specified terms.

resistance price level at which rising prices have stopped rising and either moved sideways or reversed direction; usually seen as a price chart pattern.

reversal stop a stop that, when hit, is a signal to reverse the current trading position. Also known as stop and reverse.

reversal system system in which each signal closes the previous position and opens another, opposite position.

risk of ruin chance that, using a given system or method, one will deplete one's funds to zero.

risk/reward ratio the relationship between the probability of loss and that of profit.

round lot order of shares in a multiple of 100.

R-squared percentage of variation in the dependent variable that is explained by the regression equation. A relative measure of fit.

saucer base similar to a cup-and-handle formation, but the saucer base is more shallow and rounder in shape.

scatter chart type of chart that shows price occurrences plotted against time.

secular trend trend that takes place over a long, indefinite period of time.

seed first value used to start a calculation. For example, an exponentially smoothed moving average (EMA) uses the previous day's EMA for the calculation. On the first day's calculation you could use the value of a simple moving average as the seed for the EMA.

shares outstanding shares of a corporation's stock that have been issued and are in the hands of the public.

Sharpe ratio risk-adjusted measure developed by William F. Sharpe, calculated using standard deviation and excess return to determine reward per unit of risk. The higher the Sharpe ratio, the better the historical risk-adjusted performance.

short state of having borrowed a security in order to sell it, or, in the case of a futures contract, entering into an agreement to sell a particular security at a given price at a specific time in the future.

slippage difference between the anticipated cost and the actual cost of a transaction.

spike sharp rise in price in a single bar or two.

spread the difference between the asking price and the bid price.

spread order instruction to simultaneously buy and sell the same or related commodities in an attempt to take advantage of the price differential.

standard deviation the positive square root of the expected value of the square of the difference between a random variable and its mean. The dispersion of observations from the mean observation. This measure often is expressed as a percentage on an annualized basis.

Sterling ratio (or return to drawdown or MAR ratio) ratio that compares the rate of return with the worst-case loss, thus a measurement or risk-adjusted rate of return, calculated as: (Annual ROR)/(Maximum drawdown).

stock ownership claims on a corporation's earnings and assets.

stops orders placed at a predetermined price over or under the current price of the market.

stop and reverse (SAR) stop that, when hit, is a signal to reverse the current trading position, from long to short or short to long. Also known as a reversal stop.

stop close only (SCO) a stop order that can be triggered and executed only during the market's closing range.

stop limit variation on the simple stop that instructs the filling broker to fill an order at a specified price or better, if possible, once the stop is triggered. This gives the trader more control over the fill price. If, however, the market runs the stipulated price before the broker is able to execute it, the order becomes a regular limit order. Then, if the market does not return to the specified level before the order expires, the order will not be executed.

stop limit close only (SLCO) stop limit order that can be triggered and executed only during the closing range.

stop loss risk management technique in which the trade is liquidated to halt any further decline in value.

stop with limit similar to the stop limit except that the trader must stipulate two prices with the limit price being farther away from the current market than the stop price is.

strike price see *exercise price*.

support historical price level at which falling prices have stopped falling and either moved sideways or reversed direction; usually seen as a price chart pattern.

technical analysis form of market analysis that studies supply and demand for securities and commodities based on trading price and volume studies. Using charts and modeling techniques, technicians attempt to identify price trends in a market.

tick minimum fluctuation of a tradable. For example, bonds trade in 32nds, most stocks trade in eighths, S&P 500 index trades in 5-cent increments.

ticker scrolling display of current or recent security prices and/or volume.

trading the act of buying and selling for speculation, as opposed to investing for the long term.

trading bands lines plotted in and around the price structure to form an envelope, answering whether prices are high or low and forewarning whether to buy or sell.

transform process or function for changing or converting data.

trend current general direction of movement for prices or rates.

trend channel see *channel*.

trend line straight line on a chart that shows the market's direction.

TRIN also known as the Arms index. Named after its originator, Richard Arms, this volume-based indicator looks at market strength and breadth and simply states whether the stocks gaining in price or those dropping in price are getting the greater share of market activity.

uptrend upward price movement of a security or the overall market.

volatility measure of the degree of stability of the price of a stock, index, or commodity. A highly volatile stock, one that experiences wide price swings, is considered to be more speculative than one with a low volatility.

whipsaw losing money on both sides of a price swing.

yield for a stock, the annual dividend divided by current price per share. The rate of return an investor receives if a fixed-income instrument is held to maturity.

Bibliography

Achelis, Steven B. *Technical Analysis from A to Z*. Probus Publishing, 1995.

Appel, Gerald. *The Moving Average Convergence-Divergence Method*. Great Neck, NY: Signalert, 1979.

Babcock, Bruce Jr. *Profitable Commodity Futures Trading from A to Z*. CTCR. 1994.

Balsara, Nauzer J. *Money Management Strategies for Futures Traders*. John Wiley & Sons, Inc., 1992.

Band, Richard E. *Contrary Investing*. Penguin Books, 1985.

Bernstein, Jacob. *Cyclic Analysis in Futures Trading*. John Wiley & Sons, 1988.

Bernstein, Jacob. *Short-Term Trading in Futures*. Probus Publishing Company, 1987.

Boroson, Warren. *Mutual Fund Switch Strategies & Timing Tactics*. Probus Publishing Company, 1991.

Browne, Harry. *Why the Best-Laid Investment Plans Usually Go Wrong*. William Morrow and Company, Inc., 1987.

Carolan, Christopher. *The Spiral Calendar*. New Classics Library, 1992.

Dorsey, Thomas J. *Point & Figure Charting*. John Wiley & Sons, Inc., 1995.

Dreman, David. *The New Contrarian Investment Strategy*. Random House, 1980.

Ehlers, John F. *MESA and Trading Market Cycles*. John Wiley & Sons, Inc., 1992.

Eng, William F. *The Technical Analysis of Stocks, Options & Futures*. Probus Publishing, 1988.

Epstein, Charles B. *Managed Futures in the Institutional Portfolio*. John Wiley & Sons, Inc., 1992.

Faulker, Charles. *NLP: The New Technology of Achievement*. William Morrow and Company, Inc., 1994.

Frost, A.J. and Robert Prechter. *Elliott Wave Principle*. New Classics Library, Inc., 1985.

Graham, Benjamin. *The Intelligent Investor*. Harper & Row, 1973.

Krutsinger, Joe. *The Trading Systems ToolKit*. Probus Publishing, 1994.

Lofton, Todd. *Getting Started in Futures*. John Wiley & Sons, Inc., 1989.

Mancuso, Joseph R. *How to Prepare and Present a Business Plan*. Prentice Hall Press, 1983.

Maurice, S. Charles, Owen R. Phillips and C. E. Ferguson. *Economic Analysis—Theory and Application.* Richard D. Irwin, Inc., 1982.

McMillan, Lawrence G. *Options as a Strategic Investment.* New York Institute of Finance, 1986.

Nison, Steve. *Japanese Candlestick Charting Techniques.* New York Institute of Finance, 1991.

Pardo, Robert. *Design, Testing and Optimization of Trading Systems.* John Wiley & Sons, Inc., 1992.

Salvatore, Dominick and Eugene A. Diulio. *Schaum's Outline of Theory and Problems of Principles of Economics.* McGraw-Hill, Inc., 1980.

Shimizu, Seiki. *The Japanese Chart of Charts.* Tokyo Futures Trading Publishing Company, 1986.

Slavin, Stephen L. *Economics: A Self-Teaching Guide.* John Wiley & Sons, Inc., 1988.

Stewart, James B. *Den of Thieves.* Simon & Schuster, 1991.

Stoken, Dick A. *Strategic Investment Timing.* Probus Publishing, 1990.

The Editors of *Money. Money Guide. The Stock Market.* Andrews, McMeel & Parker, 1987.

Thomsett, Michael C. *Getting Started in Options.* John Wiley & Sons, Inc., 1989.

Toppel, Edward Allen. *Zen in the Markets.* Samurai Press, 1992.

Vince, Ralph. *Portfolio Management Formulas.* John Wiley & Sons, Inc., 1990.

Wilder, J. Welles, Jr. *New Concepts in Technical Trading Systems.* Hunter Publishing Company, 1978.

Index